T0306556

VW Bus and Pick-Up: Special Models

SO (Sonderausführungen) and Special Body
Variants for the VW Transporter 1950–2010

VW Bus and Pick-Up: Special Models

SO (Sonderausführungen) and Special Body
Variants for the VW Transporter 1950–2010

David Eccles and Michael Steinke

The Crowood Press

First published in 2011 by
The Crowood Press Ltd
Ramsbury, Marlborough
Wiltshire SN8 2HR

www.crowood.com

British Library Cataloguing-in-Publication Data
A catalogue record for this book is available from the British Library.

ISBN 978 1 84797 276 7

Disclaimer
Some words, model names and designations are trademarked and are the property of the trademark holder. They have been used for identification purposes only and this is not an official publication.

While every effort has been made to ensure the accuracy of all material, the authors and publisher cannot accept liability for loss resulting from error, mis-statement, inaccuracy or omission contained herein. The authors welcome any corrections or additional information.

Photography by David Eccles.

Period materials and additional photographs courtesy of Archiv Klassische VW Transporter. Many individuals have also helped with information or supplied pictures, and thanks go to all of them for their support. In particular, credit and thanks for help, supplying additional photographs and/or archive and brochure material must be given to: Bob Amos (Portuguese Chiller Van); Graeme Booth (Swiss Postal Van); Claire Brooks (unrestored Frickinger Hearse); Guido Boes (T1 Ladder Truck); Brian Bussell (restored Australian Box Van); Graham Collin (Moortown conversions); Randy Coburn (T3 Wide Bed); Richard Copping (brochure materials and T2 Surveillance Van); Bob Davidson (SO 31); Dan Dimbleby (SO 2 Ice Cream Van); Colin Dulson (UK School Bus); Thomas Ebke (T2 Tipper); Cee Eccles (T1 Ambulance, T1 Cherry Picker, T1 SO 4); Gareth Evans (T3 Fire Support Syncro, T4 Razorback); Flash (T1 Radar Bus, T1 Ladder Truck); Julian Hunt (photographs from the Hanover 60 year anniversary event 2007); David Hyde (Swiss army vehicles); Dan Kinsey (Binz); Roland Knauss (High Roof Surveillance buses); Vince Molenaar (T2 Money Transporter and archive materials); Don McNeal (US Low Loader); Lars Neuffer (Jagdwagen); Rawdyn Nutting/Andre Hummel (Telescrambler); Alexander Prinz/Bulli Museum (T2 Police Loudspeaker Van, T2 Crane, T2 Ladder Truck, Bulli Museum buses); Andreas Plogmaker (T2 Low Loader); Richard Rowarth (Binz); Hubert Rechmann (various street scene photographs); John Weninger (Australian Container Van archive materials, Australian airport buses); Peter Valentin (Brazilian Taxi); Dave Whipp (Brainbridge Fire Truck). If anyone has inadvertently been omitted, please inform the authors so credit can be given in any reprint.

Acknowledgements
Special thanks to VW Nutzfahrzeuge, Hanover and VW Commercial, UK.

Dedication
This book is dedicated to my wife Cee, who has always loved working buses. Without her encouragement and inspiration this book would not have been written.
David

Typeset and designed by Bookcraft Ltd, Stroud, Gloucestershire

Printed and bound in China by Everbest Printing Co. Ltd

contents

ABOVE: Special Models on show in 1997 at the 50th Anniversary meet in Holland.

Wolfsburger Delikatessen van.

From the outset Volkswagen had always planned that their new Transporter would have many uses beyond that of Lieferwagen (Delivery Van). An internal memo dated 15 August 1949, after the success of the second prototype with its new unitary subframe and Kübelwagen-style reduction gears, outlined plans to build a prototype Pick-Up and Microbus, as well as a special version for the Post Office, an Ambulance, and a Panel Van. In all, eight prototypes and pre-production models were built, including a Kombi with its multi function or workhorse and people carrier appeal. With an eye on commercial sales, one of the Panel vans had three-dimensional lettering advertising itself as 'Wolfsburger

Delikatessen'. In fact the very first Panel Van to officially roll off the production line, on 8 March 1950, was delivered in primer to the Cologne dealership for the 4711 Perfume Company, which had it painted and liveried with its own colours and logos. The potential

for businesses to promote themselves by personalizing the exterior would become so successful that it was used in a special brochure, printed in June 1952, entitled *Who Drives a VW Transporter?* which was devoted to pictures of liveried and sign-written buses.

The June 1952 brochure 'Who Drives a VW Transporter?' was devoted to pictures of liveried buses and included some Special Bodies.

A Miesen Ambulance used by the Fire Service and the first Follow Me aircraft control vehicle were shown.

Amongst the liveried buses in the brochure were these pre-August 1951 laundry vans. The Boco Van is particularly interesting as it features a sliding door, with part of the body swage line and gutter smoothed to allow its operation.

One of the pre-production (note cooling vents) models featured three-dimensional lettering, with a humorous reference to the factory. This vehicle went on to be sold and was used by a bakery in Wolfsburg in the early 1950s, still with the lettering.

1951: THE FIRST SPECIAL MODELS

Interestingly, it was the dealerships and their customers who provided the impetus for Volkswagen to promote the differing ways the new Transporter could be adapted for a more specialized use than simply 'delivery'. To keep its dealerships updated with the latest Transporter models and information, from 1950 to 1965 Volkswagen produced its own in-house publication called *VW Information*. This was supplemented from 1959 to 1965 with a colour magazine entitled *Flotter Transport*, devoted to the uses and travels of the Transporter and Pick-Up. The first details of special equipment (Mehrausstattung) were carried in the November 1950 edition of *VW Information*, which published dimensions and technical data for Lieferwagen (Delivery Van) modifications that dealers might wish to offer their customers. This included special roof racks, and roof extensions and roof fitments, internal measurements, and sketches of the load area and rear wheel well to facilitate the fitting of interior panelling, dividers and insulation, as well as suggestions for sign-writing on the sides. Also described was how the dealership could fit a rear window and

an opening rear hatch, the popularity of which was such that they became factory-fitted options (M51 and M50) the following April.

The response from dealerships to the possibilities of adapting the basic model was so positive that the theme was expanded for the February/March 1951 edition of *VW Information*, which was devoted entirely to pictures, sketches and details of specific modifications and conversions carried out for customers by various dealerships over the past few months. A fascinating range of prototype Special Models was shown and described in detail. These were the forerunners of what would become a full range of Sonderausführungen.

A Kombi, owned by the Telefunken Radio Company, was adapted for use as a mobile Telefunken car radio fitting and repair service, complete with spares and measuring instruments as well as being used for training its employees. The Gottfried Schultz VW dealership, based in Essen, fully kitted out the internal load area walls of a Panel Van with wooden shelving and cubby holes for use as a VW parts Delivery Van. A similar vehicle, built at the factory for the VW Spares Department, was similarly kitted out with storage bins and shelving. Known as 'The Flying Parts Service', this vehicle was used by Volkswagen to keep their dealerships supplied with parts and to ship out urgently needed items.

The first Bread Wagon was also shown, specially converted for a bakery to supply shops with daily fresh bread. As well as the walls, all the internal load space was shelved to 'maximise 100% of the load area.' A butcher also had a Panel Van specially kitted out for selling and delivering fresh meat. As well as a shelved load area, the space above the engine compartment was also adapted to house metal storage bins, which were accessed using the opening rear hatch modification described in the November edition.

The 1955 Special Interiors brochure carried pictures of ladder and roof rack additions previously described to dealers in 1951.

Buses kitted out for bread deliveries were first shown in 1951 literature and the 1955 Special Interiors brochure showed some 1951 examples (note lack of rear bumpers).

The pictures of the Butcher's Van were shown originally in 1951 dealership information and show the opening rear hatch modification.

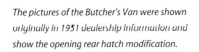

This 1951 VW parts Delivery Van, kitted out with storage bins and shelving, also featured an awning attached to the roof rack.

One particularly interesting option shown was a multi-layout metal shelving system, designed and fitted by the Willy Dost dealership of Hildesheim, which proved so successful it became marketed as a special option called the Wido system and was later given its own Volkswagen designation of SO 21 (see page 27). The system was very flexible, essentially consisting of shelving on three sides and above the load area, with bowls and storage trays. As well as offering a flexible variety of shelving and storage layouts, the system was easily removable. This edition also showed how to convert the van into a Livestock Transporter!

The first version of a specially converted Kombi for the police was also unveiled. Built for the Kiel Police Department, it was called a Mannschafts Transportwagen (Crew Transport) and featured a folding table and light attached to the front bulkhead, and a hinged flap-up dash table for the front passenger. The side and rear windows were fitted with reinforced wire mesh and there was a closed section in the rear for carrying a prisoner.

Another special model publicized was the new Ambulance conversion by the firm Miesen-Bonn, a company specializing in medical vehicles and equipment. The Kombi-based Ambulance, introduced in October 1950, retained the large 'Barndoor' tailgate but had a storage cupboard built over the engine which was accessed from the rear via a small hatch (an opening tailgate was available to special order) or from inside via a sliding door separating the load area from the rear section. Stretchers were loaded/unloaded via

The Wido multi-layout shelf system was developed by the Willy Dost dealership in late 1950.

the cargo doors – not an ideal solution! As well as a flashing light, an illuminated Red Cross sign and a siren, the Miesen version also featured two fresh air scoops on the roof and a slide-out step. Such was the popularity of this that Volkswagen went on to introduce their own specially designed factory version (Type 27), making the Miesen version no longer viable to produce.

Another specially equipped Transporter was kitted out with telephone and radio equipment, including a 10W radio for passengers, with links to landlines and phone exchanges, offering 'the dream of all VW drivers, to talk to someone in a foreign country while sitting behind the steering wheel.' And the Surveyors' Department from the Stuttgart Municipal Authority showed off their Kombi, chosen for its ability to cope with rough terrain and tracks, and fitted out as a mobile office with safe storage for theodolites and fragile surveying instruments.

Capitalizing on the response from customers and dealers, Volkswagen were proud to show off the flexible and varied commercial uses to which the new Transporter could be put, and the bulletin closed with an appeal to the dealers to think creatively about opportunities and share more ideas for future publication. To show more possibilities, they also announced a range of new forthcoming factory options, including the opening rear hatch above the engine, with or without a window, circular roof fresh air vents (M55), a canvas sliding sunroof (M87) and cargo doors on both sides (Type 21E/23E). There was also news (and a picture) of a new full-width dashboard option complete with radio and clock, though no mention was made that this would be standard on their forthcoming Deluxe Microbus.

The July 1951 *VW Information* showed off this newly introduced Deluxe Microbus, or Samba, which had gone into production on 1 June. Interestingly, it was classified as a Special Model by Volkswagen – the VW Kleinbus Sonderausführung – and it was not generally available to the public until 1952. This iconic model, with its roof windows and sliding roof options, curved corner windows and top-of-the-range trim level, has gone on to become one of the most sought

The Miesen Ambulance was introduced in October 1950.

The July 1951 VW Information introduced the new Deluxe Microbus. The demonstration vehicles featured a white roof. Note the sliding door bus in the background!

after and highly prized VW Bus models today.

Volkswagen had always had plans to produce its own Ambulance model, and the first factory Ambulance prototype was also featured in the July 1951 edition. Unlike the Miesen version, this featured a radical rear end redesign with the Barndoor engine lid replaced by a smaller version (similar to what would become standard for all models from March 1955). A new larger, opening tailgate was now able to be fitted allowing rear access for stretchers. This was hinged at the top when production commenced in December 1951 but within six months a new version, hinged at the bottom to flap down and form a supporting extension platform, had been adopted.

Inspired by the curved rear corner windows of the Deluxe, a Special Display Panel Van was depicted; as well as being used for delivery, goods could be laid out and displayed on the rear shelf above the engine and viewed via the rear tailgate window and the two curved side windows. Finally, two more factory options were announced: a sliding cargo door and a walk-through version with divided cab seats (M57).

The November 1951 dealership magazine carried yet more examples of Special Models, built and adapted for specific uses. Several of these would go

1951 publicity shot of the new Deluxe.

The rare 1951 Ambulance brochure showed the early version with top hinged tailgate; the 1952 brochure showed the revised version.

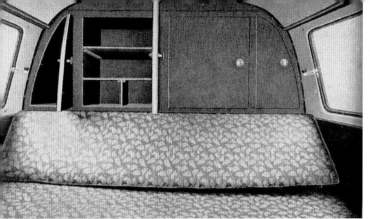

These 1951 images of a Wohnwagen show what resembles an early non-Westfalia prototype camping box interior with press stud curtains.

on to become standard SO models and widely used. The first Mobile Shop and Milk Delivery Wagon, complete with cooling equipment, was described and the first ever information about using the Transporter as a Camper was published. Described as a Wohnwagen, the factory mock-up shows what resembles an early prototype camping box interior with press stud curtains.

A Microbus fitted with sliding roof and Plexiglas roof window above the driver, complete with Follow Me signs, was shown in use as an airport control car for guiding planes into position (the first of many!) while the first Magirus TSF Fire Truck conversion, with a single side window at the rear, also featured. Other examples showing the range of ingenious uses the Transporter was specially adapted for included a radio and amplified sound broadcasting bus, a version for carrying heavy-duty electric cables, a pig/ livestock transporter with wood slat lining inside and slatted doors replacing the normal closed cargo doors, an ADAC bus designed to attend motorcycle breakdowns, and a promotional conversion by Schuh Firma featuring a huge side display window, loudspeakers and a record player attached to the passenger seat.

In just eighteen months since the introduction of the 'Box on Wheels', the VW Transporter had firmly established itself as a key player in the market. Part of this success lay not only in the range of standard models on offer, from Delivery Van to People Carrier to multi-purpose Kombi, but also in the

The 1955 brochure entitled Interior Equipment brought together a range of models specially adapted for businesses.

Now in the Stiftung AutoMuseum, Wolfsburg, this 1952 Fire Truck was one of the first Magirus converted versions, with a single window on each side and mobile pump equipment inside. The blue lights, roof rack and right mirror are later additions.

flexible and varied way these could be adapted and modified for specific uses. With the advent of the Pick-Up in August 1952, the range of possibilities, special body conversions and uses was extended even more, leading to a myriad of Special Models.

1955: *SPECIAL INTERIORS* BROCHURE

VW Information continued to profile examples of innovative adaptations and, as sales rose and interest increased, they were quick to capitalize on targeting this specialized usage

This 1952 Ambulance was converted to house a removable life support pod.

Some very early camping interiors were also shown. The bottom right image is the Westfalia demonstrator used by the Blencks to travel across South Africa.

The camping mock ups were originally exhibited at the Frankfurt Motor Show in 1952, with the doors removed to showcase the interior layouts.

This Deluxe was kitted out as a Hunter's Car for an Arabian Sheik, complete with upholstered L-shaped seating, gun racks and a striped awning tent (not a Westfalia version).

sector of the market. The versatility of the Transporter, whether Panel Van, Kombi, Microbus or Pick-Up and the variety of uses it could be put to was promoted and advertised in a 1955 brochure entitled *Special Interiors*. This brochure brought together the models featured previously in the in-house dealership magazines, depicting over thirty body variants from Pick-Up ladder trucks and glass carriers to a Life Support Pod Transporter and Mobile Cinema with projection screen. The Special Models shown are all pre-December 1953 (or pre-April 1954 in the case of the Pick-Ups), as evidenced by the lack of rear bumpers, and many are 1951/52 models with piano-hinge vent window. Some, like the Mobile Shop interior, are probably demonstration mock ups, and others are artist's impressions made to look like photographs. Some full Camping interiors were also shown, and a Samba with L-shaped lounge seating. In complete contrast to the colourful and stylish Bernd Reuter's brochure art, with its exaggerated curving lines and emotional appeal, the emphasis here was simply on the models. The layout and design is classic and uncluttered, with minimal text and lots of white space, but the use of inserts and pastel tinted backgrounds, appropriate to the model's working environment, make for an eye-catching and fascinating brochure. Volkswagen make it clear, however, that the Special Bodies and equipment shown are not factory models but that it is the VW dealerships that have the skill, expertise and contacts to 'increase the efficiency of your VW Transporter for your individual needs.'

1957: THE SO DESIGNATION IS ADOPTED

Abbreviated from Sonderausführungen, the prefix SO was initially applied to all conversions not carried out in the factory. The first official SO designations used from 1956 also carried the name of the town where the Coachbuilding Specialist was situated, for example Westfalia's SO 1 Mobile Shop was suffixed with Wiedenbrück, the Binz SO 16 with Lorch, and SO 12 with Minden. In late 1957 the first official listing of the most popular Sonderausführungen (Special Models) was made available for dealerships, with each model identified with a number and SO prefix and information. Some of these SO models were offered by the VW factory; others were converted or modified by specialist Karosserie baufirma. Technical information,

specifications and options, as well as details of the relevant conversion company, were included in the listings. The following models were listed as available, including new SO designations for Westfalia Campers.

- SO 1 Mobile Shop conversion
- SO 3/4 Police Accident and Command vehicles
- SO 5 Insulated Cold Transport Van (with dry-ice fan blower and 140mm insulating board)
- SO 6 Insulated Cold Transport Van (80mm insulating board)
- SO 7 Refrigerated Freezer Van
- SO 8 Wide Bed Pick-Up (metal)
- SO 9 Wide Bed Pick-Up (wood)
- SO 11 Pick-Up Ladder Truck
- SO 12 Pick-Up Box Wagon with aluminium roll shutter doors
- SO 13 Pick-Up with enclosed storage box
- SO 14 pole-carrying trailer (wheeled base only, no storage) and mounting for load bed

- SO 15 Tipper Truck
- SO 16 Binz Double Cab conversion
- SO 18 Mobile workshop/breakdown truck
- SO 19 Display/Exhibition Bus
- SO 21 Wido multi-layout shelving
- SO 22 Westfalia camping box
- SO 23 Westfalia Deluxe camping model
- SO 24 Trailer and mounting for Pick-Up bed for carrying long poles/pipes
- SO 29 Red Cross emergency/ disaster trailer unit
- SO 30 Drag Sled stretcher for use in mines
- SO 32 Enclosed Box Van similar to SO 12 but with roll shutter access.

As a model or conversion such as a Double Cab became a production line model in the Hanover plant it lost the SO number and was given an M code instead to show body conversion. These numbers were then allocated to another conversion, as in the

This 1967 brochure depicted a full range of SO and special body variants.

case of SO 8 and SO 9 Wide Bed Pick-Ups. From 1960 the newly introduced Cherry Picker carried SO 8, SO 9 and a new SO 10, depending on height of lifting platform.

From 1960 to 1964 a very special promotional tour took place. The VW Caravan, known as the VW Transporter Sonderschau, toured cities and dealerships showing off the latest models. Special Models were a central part of this and included a Tipper, Shops, Emergency vehicles and Ladder Truck as well as new models of Cherry Picker and Low Loader Pick-Up conversions. So successful were these special body options, that in 1963 *Flotter Transport* showcased eighty different variants, stating, 'VW Commercials a la carte, which type would you like? Here is a menu giving you 80 possibilities, from the standard models produced in the factory, to the Special Models produced in Germany by firms recommended to us.'

1962: VW COMMERCIALS EQUIPPED FOR MANY PURPOSES

Although not specifically named as a Special Models brochure, this uninspiringly named brochure was multi-lingual and aimed to demonstrate the versatility of the VW Transporter and Pick-Up, and their many uses, stating, 'This catalogue will show you just how ingenious some customers were in adapting their VW Commercials to suit the particular requirements of their own business … your VW dealer has got a full range of literature giving details of these Special Models just waiting here for you.' With an eye on export sales, examples from other countries were shown, and some of the 51 Barndoor models previously shown in the 1955 brochure were still included.

1963: REVISED SO LISTING

From 1963, dealership catalogues carried a revised SO listing with the following amendments/inclusions:

- SO 2 High Roof Mobile Shop conversion
- SO 6II 80mm insulating board Cold Transport Van
- SO 6III Refrigerated Meat Transport Van

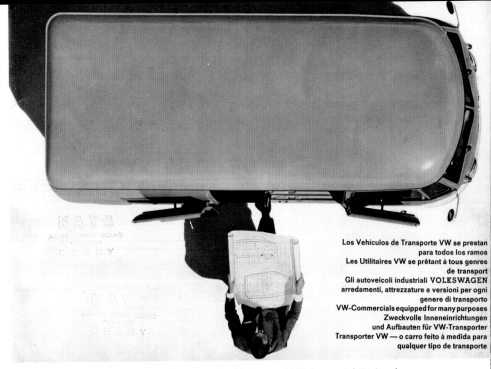

Los Vehículos de Transporte VW se prestan para todos los ramos
Les Utilitaires VW se prêtant à tous genres de transport
Gli autoveicoli industriali VOLKSWAGEN arredamenti, attrezzature e versioni per ogni genere di trasporto
VW-Commercials equipped for many purposes
Zweckvolle Inneneinrichtungen und Aufbauten für VW-Transporter
Transporter VW — o carro feito à medida para qualquer tipo de transporte

The 1962 multi-lingual Commercials brochure was uninspiringly named 'VW Commercials Equipped for Many Purposes'.

Interiors used by butchers, bakers and mobile grocers demonstrated a range of shop uses.

The 1951 Follow Me Van shown in 1951, 1952 and 1955 made another appearance in 1962!

This Panel Van equipped for use by a travelling salesman (possibly haberdashery) featured a bolt-on roof rack and side access flap. The truck mirrors show it to be a US Bus.

VW-Pritschenwagen mit Jalousie-Aufbau

Hersteller:
Firma Felix Striepke
2301 Schönwohld üb. Kiel, Post Russee, Tel. Achterwehr 348

Brutto-Verkaufspreis:
ab Schönwohld bei freier Anlieferung des Fahrzeuges

1. Grundmodell:
VW-Pritschenwagen 261, serienmäßig lackiert
M 57 Bodenleisten lose beigelegt   ohne Mehrpreis
M 118 ohne Bordwände   DM 140,—

2. Ausstattung:
Jalousie-Aufbau   DM 1332,80

Versandkosten:
Auslieferung Hannover—Kiel   DM 107,—
Entladen und Überführen
von Kiel nach Schönwohld   DM 25,—
Überführen von Schönwohld
nach Kiel und Verladen   DM 25,—
Fracht von Kiel zum Bestimmungsort   je nach Entfernung

Nutzlast   875 kg

Abnahme durch den TÜV ist vor der Zulassung erforderlich.
Gebühren: DM 30,—.

Hinweise:
Die Firma Felix Striepke fertigt einen Jalousie-Aufbau, der aus Stirnwand, Rückwand und Dach besteht. Auf der linken und rechten Seite sind je zwei abschließbare Jalousien angebracht.
Sowohl die Stirnwand als auch die Rückwand bestehen aus 3,5 mm starken Hartfaserplatten, die außen mit Stahlblech (Stärke 0,8 mm) überzogen sind. Das aus Holzsprießeln und -leisten bestehende Dach ist mit schwarzem Kunstleder bespannt und ringsum mit einer polierten Alu-Regenleiste versehen. Der Pritschenboden wird mit einer 3,5 mm starken Hartfaserplatte bedeckt. Während die Holm- und Führungsleisten aus Hartholz — Buche beziehungsweise Esche — gefertigt werden, bestehen die Jalousieleisten aus nordischer Kiefer. Die Jalousieleisten werden vor ihrem Zusammenbau einmal geölt und einmal farblos lackiert. Nach dem Zusammenbau wird die Jalousie ein zweites Mal lackiert.
Gegen einen entsprechenden Mehrpreis fertigt der Hersteller auf Wunsch auch Zwischenwände aus Hartfaserplatten und Holzregale an (siehe Abbildung).
Der genannte Preis schließt eine Lackierung des Aufbaus in einer der VW-Transporter-Serienfarben (gewünschte Farbe angeben) ein. Für die grundfarbige Ausführung beträgt der Minderpreis DM 40,—.
Der Aufbau muß im Betrieb der Firma Striepke montiert werden.

The 1963 Anregungen listing, designed to show ideas and possibilities, included this roll shutter sides Box Van, formerly listed as SO 12.

- SO 8 Pick-Up (Cherry Picker) with hydraulic lifting platform V90 (largest size)
- SO 9 Pick-Up with smaller hydraulic lifting platform V80 (Cherry Picker)
- SO 10 Pick-Up with single person hydraulic lifting platform V60
- SO 25 Pick-Up Low Loader
- SO 31 Heating Oil Delivery Pick-Up with tank and dispenser pump.

From 1963 the Wido system was listed simply as an option, not as SO 21.

By 1964 the dealership catalogues had SO variants grouped according to base model, so, for example, all Pick-Up variants followed details of the factory base model and option. Grouped under Kombi, Westfalia Campers were included with SO 33 (installed Camping Mosaik 22 kit) and Flipseat models SO 34/35 for 1961–65, and SO 42/44 and SO 45 (Camping Mosaik kit) for 1965–67. SO 36 referred to the fitting of the Martin Walter Dormobile roof.

ANREGUNGEN (SUGGESTIONS)

To further show the versatility of the Volkswagen, each model listing now also carried a range of sketches, artist's impressions and mock-up photographs showing different possibilities for adapting a model. Details of firms able to carry out such conversions were provided. Grouped as Anregungen ('Suggestions'), they included one offs or suggestions and ideas designed to get a customer thinking specifically about their own individual needs. Previous SO-designated Pick-Ups with box containers (SO 12 and so on) were now all listed under Anregungen, with a variety of different bodies from drinks delivery to livestock transport.

BAY WINDOW SO MODEL CODES

Working in partnership with its specialist companies, the factory-approved SO designation continued into the Bay Window models, with a slightly trimmed listing:

- SO 1 Mobile Shop conversion
- SO 2 High Roof Mobile Shop conversion
- SO 3 Police Accident and Command vehicles

Lattenrost-Wandverkleidung

Oftmals werden auch wenige Latten die Laderaumwand aus-
reichend schützen.

Hinweise über die Montage von Schutzleisten für VW-Transporter finden Sie in der Technischen Mitteilung A 5 des VW-
Kundendienstes.

VW-Kastenwagen für den Kleinvieh-Transport

Zur intensiveren Belüftung des Fahrzeugs wurde die Zweiflügeltür in eine Lattentür umgebaut.

Um das Herausspringen der Tiere bei geöffneter Tür zu ver-
meiden, wurden zusätzlich einhängbare Lattenverschläge angebracht.

VW-Kastenwagen für den Kleinvieh-Transport

Bei diesem Fahrzeug handelt es sich um einen VW-Kasten-
wagen mit Türen beidseitig und elektrischer Standbelüftung
(M 121). Die Türen wurden zur intensiveren Belüftung des
Laderaums mit zusätzlichen Lüftungsschlitzen versehen. Das
hintere Fenster wurde durch ein Holzgitter ersetzt. Die Inneneinrichtung (Holz) teilt den Laderaum in 5 Transport-Boxen
ein.

The Livestock Transporter first shown in 1951 and another closed-door version were also shown as Anregungen.

BELOW: *SO 15 Tipper Trucks were normally Single Cab conversions; the Doka (Double Cab) version seen here was a special order.*

- SO 5 Insulated Cold Transport Van (with dry-ice fan blower and 140mm insulating board)
- SO 6II Insulated Cold Transport Van (80mm insulating board)
- SO 6III Refrigerated Meat Transport Van
- SO 7 Refrigerated Freezer Van
- SO 8 Pick-Up (Cherry Picker) with hydraulic lifting platform V90 (largest size)
- SO 9 Pick-Up with smaller hydraulic lifting platform V80 (Cherry Picker)
- SO 10 Pick-Up with single person hydraulic lifting platform V60
- SO 11 Pick-Up Ladder Truck
- SO 12 Pick-Up Box Wagon with aluminium roll shutter doors
- SO 13 Pick-Up with enclosed storage box
- SO 14 pole-carrying trailer and mounting for Pick-Up Bed for carrying long poles/pipes
- SO 15 Tipper Truck
- SO 24 Box Trailer and mounting for long loads
- SO 25 Pick-Up Low Loader.

Westfalia Campers continued to receive the SO designation, and from 1969 had an additional digit and city name to show layout and fitments, for example SO 73/1, Düsseldorf. Interestingly, by the mid 1970s SO 76 was simply known either as the Berlin or the Helsinki (depending on layout configuration), unlike SO 42 or SO 72 which are still referred to and best known by their SO designation.

By now many other companies were also producing a full range of specialist body conversions, notably the Pon dealership in Holland, and Belgian company D'Ieteren, which made a range of Special Bodies marketed as De Winkel Fleet. The 'unofficial' SO models listed included a Snow Plough, Ladder Truck, Refrigerated vehicles, Glass Transport Truck, Dustcart, Street Cleaner, Tipper Truck and Market Garden Produce Delivery Van.

1979: SONDERAUSFÜHRUNGEN BECOME SONDERFAHRZEUGE (SPECIAL VEHICLES)

With the introduction of the T3 in 1979 the SO prefix was dropped. Instead, a list of Special Models available to order and conversion company details was provided for dealers, entitled Sonder-fahrzeuge (special vehicles). This included Westfalia's Joker Campers, Refrigerated vehicles, Ladder Trucks, Cherry Pickers, Mobile Shops and specialist delivery conversions and so on. Volkswagen did produce a few specialist market models, such as the Jagdwagen or Hunter's Car (*see* page 120), but mainly it left the manufacture and conversion for specialist use to others, concentrating on production of base models and a full range of factory options. By the mid 1980s it even stopped producing its own factory Ambulance, preferring to outsource and send base vehicles to firms such as Miesen and Binz. This has carried through to the T4 and T5; while there continue to be a myriad of different specialist uses to which they are put, these conversions are all carried out by established firms, with Volkswagen occasionally commissioning a prototype demonstrator, such as the Pick-Up Razorback (*see* page 113). From the T4 on Volkswagen also supplied a Pick-Up with rear chassis only, allowing Karosserie to coachbuild their own Special Bodies.

TOP: *The Ruthmann Steiger Cherry Picker, formerly SO 8, has continued to be built across all generations. This version is a 1982 T3.*

CENTRE: *High Roof models have always been popular for use as Ice Cream Vans.*

BELOW: *Publicity shot of a T4 Pick-Up with long load-carrying trailer similar to the SO 14 set up.*

This LT base Doka Tipper, converted by Meiller, has a steel load bed that can tip in three directions!

SIXTY YEARS OF SPECIAL MODELS

Volkswagen has continued its tradition of promoting the versatility and adaptability of the Transporter for its latest generation, the T5. Sixty years on, the looks and engineering may have changed but the message stays the same:

Volkswagen Commercial vehicles come in a range of shapes and sizes, and with a host of options and extras. It means you should have no trouble finding the perfect fit for your business. But sometimes your job is so specialist, or your requirements so specific, that you need something a little different. A little extra special. And that's where conversions come in. A conversion is a vehicle that's tailored to your exact needs. Built by our accredited converters to the highest of standards, it'll do the job you require of it, right down to the last nut and bolt. So whether it's a Tipper or Glass Carrier, an Ambulance or Curtain-side you need, you'll find it here.

This book brings together some of the many SO and special body conversions based on the VW Bus, Transporter and Pick-Up over the past sixty years. Throughout its five generations, the VW Bus has proved itself the market leader in offering businesses the perfect vehicle designed, as stated back in 1955, 'to increase the efficiency of your VW Transporter for your individual needs.'

Special body conversions on the new Crafter range include Tipper Truck and Dropside load carriers.

The Crafter range also includes Box Delivery Van conversions with Luton over cab.

This T5 Recovery vehicle, based on a Double Cab, can be raised in the middle to allow easier loading.

The Pick-Up continues to be a popular base for conversion, as in this T5 Street Cleaner produced by Pfau, with cleaning fluids carried on the load bed.

Authors' Note
Although Westfalia Campers were included in SO catalogues and listings, with SO designations for each model introduced from 1959 to 1979, they have not been included in this book, as that is another story, and a book of its own.

delivery vehicles

ABOVE: An archive photograph from the 1960s shows a fleet of bread delivery vans used by the Fork Bakery, Bochum, ready to be loaded up, including a High Roof model. Note the rotary roof ventilators.

Initially designed specifically for transporting goods, the Lieferwagen (Delivery Van) quickly became popular with businesses. Its versatile and accessible large cargo space meant it could be adapted to carry all sorts of loads and, by 1951, Volkswagen was promoting tailor-made commercial use in its dealership literature. Panel Vans were described and shown with specially adapted shelving, storage bins, body modifications and fitments individually geared to the needs and requirements of specific businesses. These included bakery and butchers vans, livestock transport, parts delivery, telecommunications and broadcast vehicles and even a mobile bathroom fitments supplier. The 1955 *Special Interiors* brochure showcased a variety of these uses, and commercial brochures since then have continued promoting the Transporter in a variety of working delivery roles and commercial applications.

This image showing a 1951 Livestock Transporter first appeared in the 1951 *Dealership Information*, and was used again for the 1955 brochure. Note the open wood slat cargo doors and two-tier accommodation.

1951 Livestock Transporter with wood slat cargo doors.

The 1962 Commercial Uses brochure showed a variety of uses such as Mobile Shops, and cake, pie and bread delivery.

Clothing and garment manufacturers also made extensive use of Panel Vans fitted with hanging rails.

By the time of the T3 the Pick-Up based Box Delivery Vans had evolved into coachbuilt versions.

KOFFER- AUFBAU

As well as basic Panel Vans, versions of the Delivery Van with an enclosed box container known as Koffer-Aufbau (literally suitcase vans), were built onto a Pick-Up base. Designated SO 12, SO 13 and SO 32, these consisted of a box container and were available with a range of doors including roll shutter sides and could be adapted to specific requirements. These models are covered with the Pick-Up variants on page 100.

By the time of the T3, these had evolved into coachbuilt versions and the new VW LT was introduced, with the new generation Crafter and T5 High Roofs taking over for today's light delivery vehicles requiring a large load capacity.

SO 5 Cold Transport Van with dry-ice blower.

SO 5/6/7 COLD TRANSPORT AND REFRIGERATED VANS

These were all converted by Firma Auto-Dunker of Friedberg, which specializes in fitting freezer and chiller equipment. Removable wood slat flooring, side step and a load area dividing shelf were commonly specified options for all models. As well as for commerce and food transport, Refrigerated vehicles were also used extensively by the National Blood Service.

SO 5 INSULATED COLD TRANSPORT VAN (140mm insulating board and dry-ice blower)

This model was a Chiller Van with dry-ice cold blower fan, capable of maintaining an internal temperature below freezing. It was well insulated and clad inside with 140mm thick insulation board. Early versions retained the original cargo doors with access to the inner sealed cold area via another internal door. From 1963 the cargo doors were replaced with a single small insulation clad door and rear access also sealed with another door inside the tailgate. The dry-ice fan blower was sited in the rear load area above the engine.

SO 6II COLD TRANSPORT VAN (80mm insulating board)

This was a basic Cold Transport Van, with the load area clad in 80mm insulation board. The existing cargo doors and tailgate provided access but were also lined. A removable metal shelf extended from the height of the rear load area to the front bulkhead, making for a large flat space.

SO 6III REFRIGERATED VAN FOR MEAT TRANSPORT

Very similar to SO 6II, this model was designed specifically for transporting meat by butchers and abattoirs and featured heavy-duty interior lining.

SO 7 REFRIGERATED FREEZER VAN

This version was the full freezer Delivery Van, featuring a sealed inner compartment with half the rear load area closed off, with an internal temperature of −24 degrees. Access was via an insulated, square side door and the generator, used to keep air chilled below freezing, was powered from the engine and sited in the load area above the engine. From around 1961–63 this also featured three blackout mesh vent 'windows' in the tailgate and a small blackout window at each upper rear side.

SO 6 was an insulated chilled goods transport vehicle.

Ventilation was provided for the refrigeration unit via meshed openings in the tailgate and upper rear sides.

SO 7 was the full freezer van with refrigeration unit.

ABOVE: The Blood Transfusion Service made extensive use of SO 7 conversions for delivering blood to hospitals.

LEFT: 1973 Auto Dunker SO 7 conversion. An insulated side access door, with heavy-duty hinges, is sited in the closed sliding door panel. RIGHT: A similar access door is sited in the tailgate. This vehicle ended up as the refrigerated larder for an Alpine roadside cafe.

This picture shows a 1985 factory demonstration Refrigerated Delivery Van. The refrigeration unit is sited on top of the van creating more internal space.

The Transporter has continued to be an ideal platform for Refrigerated vehicles. This T4 cold transport version has a temperature control unit on the roof rear.

THE SERVICE REFRIGERATION VAN

Here is the ideal in refrigeration transport with a compressor-type freezing unit. Stationary—the built-in electric motor is connected to the local power supply On the move — the unit is driven by the vehicle's engine through a countershaft. The refrigeration installation in this vehicle has been designed, like the Volkswagen itself, to give the basic needs of reliability, endurability and simplicity All ancillary fittings are of proprietary make, international repute and easily obtained.

£1195

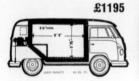

MOBILE REFRIGERATION. During road operation drive is from the VW power unit, the compressor working continuously At its depot a mains electric motor drives the compressor and is of course controlled by the thermostat. A special feature is the heated door rebate to prevent icing up of door
CAPACITY is 80 cu. ft. with side loading. The compartment is of cubical shape. No curves means maximum space utility
COMPRESSOR. Martin Bitzer unit giving 7,800 B.T U. at 30° F
MOTOR. Capacitor start single phase 230 250V Crompton Parkinson, speed 1425 rpm.
COUNTER SHAFT. Assembly incorporates a special Centrifugal Clutch which cuts out engine drive at low rpm, or when electric motor is running.

The Service Refrigeration Van utilized a compressor-type freezing unit.

THE SERVICE INSULATED VAN

Ideal for local delivery runs. Specification as The Refrigeration Van but equipped with " Drikold " refrigeration, This unit gives additional capacity (up to 85 cu. ft.) and allows access to the extra room by means of a rear door

£865

TEMPERATURES. The equipment maintains suitable temperatures for the storage and transport of frozen goods requiring Zero F conditions.
VAN INSULATION. Double layer 2in. Polystyrene, treble layer 2in. on roof.
VAN LINING. Galvanised sheet steel or aluminium.
VAN FLOOR. Water-tight sheet galvanised steel with drain hole.
DEFROSTING, maintains efficiency and is simple and swift, moisture being easily drained through drain hole.

The above specifications apply to both conversions.

The Service Insulated Van was ideally suited for local chilled deliveries.

SERVICE REFRIGERATED DELIVERY VANS

Service was a UK-based firm, best known for its camping conversion called the Mota-Caravan. Service Garages however didn't restrict its activities to the Mota-Caravan, but also offered its own versions of 'Sonderausführungen'. As well as a Mobile Shop and an Ice Cream Van (*see* Chapter 9), the range included two vehicles for transporting cold goods.

The Refrigeration Van utilized a compressor-type freezing unit, which, if the vehicle was stationary, could be plugged into the local supply. On the move, however, the unit was driven by the vehicle's engine through a countershaft.

The Service Insulated Van version was ideally suited to local delivery runs through its reliance on 'Drikold refrigeration'. Both vans were insulated with a double layer of two-inch thick Polystyrene which was increased to triple standards for the roof. The vans were lined with galvanized sheet steel or aluminium. The compressor on the Refrigeration Van prevented the window hatch above the engine being opened, whereas the insulated local Delivery Van featured rear access via the tailgate.

SO 21 WIDO MULTI-LAYOUT SHELVING SYSTEM

Very soon after the launch of the Transporter in March 1950, the Willy Dost dealership of Hildesheim offered a patent design multi-layout metal shelving system, which was so successful that in February 1951 Volkswagen published pictures and information in its dealership magazine. The system consisted of shelving and storage units which could be fitted, in various arrangements, on all three sidewalls and the load area. Taking its name from the dealership, the Wido system was given the designation SO 21 in early SO listings, though by 1963 this designation was dropped and the system shown under 'Anregungen' (suggestions).

The 1958 Wido sales brochure even illustrated how the shelving system could double as sleeping bunks, allowing the Delivery Van to be a weekend Camper.

BELOW: The Wido system remained in use during the T3 generation.

1958 Wido brochure showing a range of uses including camping.

1967 SO 7: PORTUGUESE HIGH ROOF REFRIGERATED VAN

This High Roof model was delivered to the Gel Mar frozen fish delivery firm in Portugal. The M plate shows it was built on 18 May 1967 and finished in Pearl White. Apart from the standard freezer van options of no upper vents in the load area and a windowless tailgate, it was also fitted with factory safaris, a large oil bath air cleaner (for dusty conditions) and a low compression engine (for poor grade petrol) for conditions in its future destination. Discovered in storage in 2009, it has been rescued and bought by Bob and Kate Amos of Strawberry Leisure, who plan to restore it for use with their wedding function fleet and business, though not as a freezer van!

RIGHT: A windowless tailgate was standard for chiller vans and a new access door was fitted inside.

FAR RIGHT: When closed, temperatures below freezing were maintained.

BELOW TOP: The whole inside was fully clad in wipe clean aluminium.

BELOW BOTTOM: The van was originally used by the Gel Mar frozen fish delivery firm and its logos and signwriting are still visible.

BELOW RIGHT: The BBC script badge on the tailgate is the logo of the chilling machine manufacturer.

TOP LEFT: The existing cargo doors were welded shut and a new small access door fitted.

TOP RIGHT: The inside was fully lined and insulated and the access doors given additional insulated cladding.

AUSTRALIAN BOX DELIVERY/ CONTAINER VAN

From 1962 VW Australia produced its own version of a Box Delivery Van. Unlike the Hanover-built SO 12, which had an enclosed steel box built onto a Pick-Up base, the Australian version was built on a unitized construction platform of the Panel Van.

The box section was made with a steel construction and had a payload capacity of 7 cubic metres compared to the standard Panel Van's 5 cubic metres, plus greater headroom with an overall internal floor to ceiling height of 1.8 metres. The large side panels were pressed by Ansair of Melbourne and assembled at Volkswagen Special Bodies Department within the Clayton Victoria plant, which also fabricated the new, straight rear bumper. With the exception of the four rows of timber slatting fitted along the inside of the side panels, the body was of an all steel construction and was fully welded to the cab section, forming a completely weather-proof rear area. Access was via double opening doors at the rear and twin side doors which utilized the locks from the Panel Van.

VW Australia only built one hundred and twenty-three Container Vans in total, with the last two rolling off the Clayton production line in August 1968. Despite being popular with courier companies and delivery fleets, they were much more expensive than standard models; only a handful have survived in original condition.

This quirky 1967 publicity shot shows the versatility of the Container Van perfectly.

VW Container Van

The Container Van takes a 1508 lb. load in its big, square, 240 cu. ft. space. Loading's easy because the double-opening side doors are 63.5" high x 42" wide, rear doors 44" x 56.5". Inside height, 72".

The Container Van doesn't only carry a lot of goods, it carries them efficiently. The side doors are at kerb height and the rear door at dock height—making loading and unloading quick and easy.

Every way, you save—on initial cost, oil, petrol, maintenance and repairs. Your small outlay goes further. The all-steel body is welded to the cab to form an integral dust and weather proof unit.

Both driver and cargo ride easily. With the engine in the back and the driver in front, the load is cradled in the middle. The heated and ventilated cab seats three comfortably.

1967 brochure image.

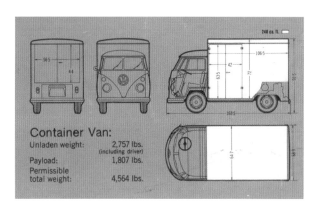

Container Van:

Unladen weight:	2,757 lbs. (including driver)
Payload:	1,807 lbs.
Permissible total weight:	4,564 lbs.

Dimensions and payload were clearly shown in brochure materials.

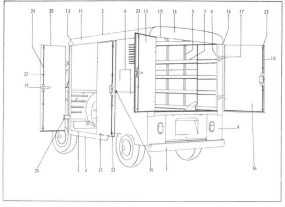

The dealership catalogue included this cut-away diagram showing key selling features to emphasize.

delivery vehicles

1968 Dutch brochure cover carries the VW logo.

The door access arrangement of the Bestelwagen (Box Delivery Van) is shown in the brochure as well as information about its load capacity and construction.

The Kemperink was also available as a Pick-Up.

KEMPERINK CONVERSIONS

Kemperink is a Dutch family firm, founded in the 1890s. By 1931 it was an established coach-building convertor. Responding to a demand for more load-carrying space, in 1954 it produced a long wheelbase-enclosed Delivery Van conversion with rear and side access, which doubled the interior load space to 10 cubic metres. The first customer was a mattress manufacturer in Rotterdam. This was followed by a fleet order from Bolletje Biscuits. The Bolletje Biscuit Delivery Vans were such a common sight in Holland that the model became known simply as 'Bolletje Bus'. C&A stores also had a fleet of Kemperinks and the Dutch army made extensive use of them for personnel transport and radio vans, as well as a special version adapted to act as mobile field kitchen with serving flap and counter.

A standard Pick-Up model was used to make the two model versions – the Bestelwagen (Box Delivery Van) and an extended bed Pick-Up (a Double Cab version was available to order). Side windows could be ordered for the Bestelwagen, and the enclosed carrying space was fabricated from a square section tubular steel frame with steel sides. The roof section was made of fibreglass. T1 Kemperinks had a flat roof profile with rounded edges, while Bay Window models had a bowed roof profile, giving extra headroom. For a less utilitarian look, chrome trim was fitted at gutter and cab door swage line height, breaking the run of flat metal. Early vehicles had twin (or single) opening side doors and (usually) a very large rear door fitted with gas struts, with roll shutter doors as an option. Later vehicles featured the option of a sliding door which was designated the 'Bestelwagen Special'. As well as new chassis member sections, the extended bed meant the new cables and brake lines also had to be specially made. These proved subject to wear and so Kemperinks were supplied with spare cables!

In 1959 Volkswagen gave official approval to the Kemperink conversion and produced its own brochures featuring the conversion. It could be ordered from dealerships and carried full Volkswagen warranty. With the introduction of Volkswagen's own long wheelbase transporter (the LT), demand for the Kemperink fell away, and production ceased in late 1979. Altogether about 2,000 vehicles of all types were produced, with approximately half of those being T1 (Split Screen) models.

For a less utilitarian look, chrome trim was fitted at gutter and cab door swage line height, breaking the run of flat metal.

ABOVE: *Another version featured a Luton-style top over the cab area, as on this sign-written Kemperink spotted at Vanfest. It also has twin vertical windows at the rear.*

RIGHT: *This rare example is one of two RHD versions produced specifically for exhibition at the Earls Court Motor Show in 1974. Like most surviving Kemperinks, it has been turned into a Camper.*

1958 MILCH BULLI

This June 1958 Panel Van (#354874) was exported to Switzerland where it was converted into a milk collection and delivery van by AMAG (Automobil und Motoren-AG), the Swiss VW dealership and importer.

The vehicle was owned and operated by ACV (Allgemeiner Consumverein), a cooperative organization founded in 1884 in Basel, and the main supplier/distributor of milk in Switzerland. The vehicle here is one of the ACV fleet, carrying the number 178, although there were, apparently, only ten such Volkswagen Panel Van conversions.

Two roof hatches give access to the main milk storage tank sited just behind the front bulkhead. This in turn feeds two dispensing compartments, one on each side, with roll-up compartment doors. The interior is fully lined for cooling, with sheet metal to cover. The load area is on two levels and accessed by a roll-up compartment door on one side and a similar door on the other that also has a fold-down door/step for standing churns and such on. The rear tailgate was replaced by another roll-up door for access at the rear to more cool storage. Milk could thus be both collected from suppliers and distributed to customers (at the time of use unpasteurized milk was still the norm). The two glass milk dispensers dispense the same capacity as the bottles hold – no spillage! During hot weather deliveries had to be made very early in the morning and driving the vehicle, apparently, called for great skill – especially on bends when the milk tank was full!

Very little is known about the actual history of the bus, except that it was finally stored for twenty years in a garage and then occasionally used as

TOP: The vehicle was converted in 1958 by AMAG for use as a fresh milk delivery van for the ACV Dairy in Switzerland.

CENTRE: It was designed to collect milk fresh from farms and then deliver it direct to the public (unpasteurized milk was the norm then).

BELOW: Roll-up metal doors on each side reveal storage and milk dispenser.

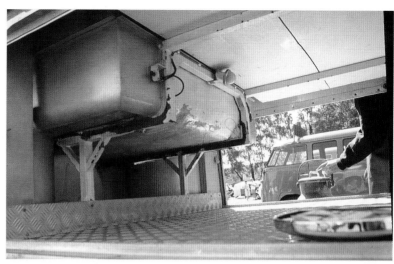

ABOVE: The glass milk dispensers dispense the same capacity as the bottles.

TOP RIGHT: The main milk storage tank, which feeds the dispensers, is sited just behind the front bulkhead.

RIGHT: The rear tailgate was replaced by another roll-up door for access at the rear to more cool storage.

a promotional vehicle by the dairy before passing into the collection of enthusiast Dieter Schmidt-Lorenz. Everything, including the engine, is completely original and unrestored, and it is now occasionally seen at special events like Bad Camberg. (The stickers on the side and rear are not original livery and refer to Dieter's VW parts business.)

BELOW: Two roof hatches give access to the main milk storage tank sited just behind the front bulkhead.

RIGHT: The interior is fully lined for cooling, with sheet metal to cover. The load area is on two levels and accessed by a roll shutter door and also has a fold-down door/step for standing churns on.

delivery vehicles

1965 BEERTRUCK

This High Roof Delivery Van was used by a dairy in Helmstedt, who originally used it to sell fresh milk to customers straight from churns. The dairy modified the cargo doors, cutting them in half, with the top halves then welded together and hinged so one large door now opened upwards and outwards, leaving the lower halves as standard side hinged doors.

Sometime in the late 1960s, it passed to a local drinks merchant, Rudolph, who held the local brewery franchise in the nearby Braunschweig area. He had the vehicle repainted in Ruby Red and sign written to advertise his business. During the week it was used to deliver beer, but at weekends it was used to sell beer direct to the public at Bierfests and events. The word 'Schankmobil' translates as 'mobile draught beer'.

Built in 1965, the van was originally used by a dairy, which carried out the modifications to the doors.

In the late 1960s it was bought by a local brewery merchant, Rudolph, who had it repainted and sign-written for his business.

LEFT: The cargo doors have been cut in half and the top halves then welded together and hinged, so one large door now opens upwards and outwards.
RIGHT: The lower door halves operate as standard side hinged doors.

MONEY TRANSPORTERS

From 1969 an armoured Money Transporter was available from Wilhelm Thiele, featuring bullet-proof glass, 3mm sheet metal lining and supplementary push locks. Bischoff & Hamel, a Hanover VW dealership, produced a more sophisticated version with short-wave radio communication, electromagnetic door locks, armour-plated doors with manual and electromagnetic locks, four pane bullet-proof glass, with steel lining and electrostatic flocking. The sliding door was replaced with a new revolving door, which could only be opened from the inside.

Another version of the Money Transporter was built exclusively for South America and commissioned by the Hamburg branch of VW Interamericana, which handled all imports to that area. An estimated fifteen to twenty of these on both early and later Bay Window platforms were ordered up to 1973. As well as sliding door access, another small door cut into the sliding one could be used. A small reinforced window was also inserted on each side and in the tailgate. Featuring steel armour plating and bullet-proof glass, it also had a warning siren on the roof and electric fresh air ventilator. However, the most distinctive feature is the steel special protection fitted to each wheel.

BELOW LEFT: A small reinforced window was also inserted on each side and in the tailgate.
RIGHT: Armoured transport for valuables is now more sophisticated, with coachbuilt bodies as in this T4 example built by Stoof of Berlin. Described as a 'safe on wheels', Stoof only used the front end of the VW, fitting their own rear chassis and axle. The 'small fortress' was low enough to access underground service areas, basements and car parks.

Bischoff & Hamel armoured Money Transporter in action.

Around fifteen to twenty of these armoured transporters were ordered for South America by VW Interamericana. Note the (removable) special wheel protection.

Featuring steel armour plating and bulletproof glass, it also had a warning siren on the roof and electric fresh air ventilator.

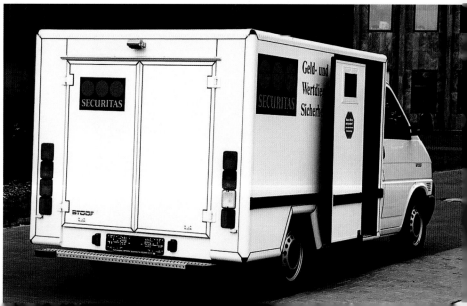

1978 BISCHOFF & HAMEL MONEY TRANSPORTER

Built in September 1978, this Bischoff & Hamel Money Transporter was delivered to Kiel and used on Pellworm Island, off the west coast of the state of Schleswig-Holstein, by 'Sparkasse Pellworm' (Pellworm savings bank). Originally finished in Neptune Blue, on the roof under the white paint it now wears, are two large joined circles, the German sign of a Money Transporter so it was recognizable from the sky. It left the factory with a host of extras including a lockable cap for the fuel tank, a lockable engine compartment lid, twin electrical fresh air ventilators, a rear hatch without window, under chassis reinforcing plates, a Blaupunkt Salzgitter FM radio, heavy-duty shocks, and battery and generator and suppression equipment prepared for radio traffic. M712 shows it was factory-prepared for conversion to an armoured Money Transporter, which included omitting parts that would be removed in the conversion such as the windows, window mechanisms, original upholstered door panels, regular rear view mirrors.

This 1978 version was used by the Pellworm savings bank, and was originally Neptune Blue.

The sliding door was replaced with a new revolving door, which could only be opened from the inside.

BELOW LEFT: The armoured plating is mounted on the inside of the vehicle with only the fixed cab windows and security mountings for the windscreen hinting at its use.

RIGHT: A small roof hatch, which is armoured and can be locked from the inside, supplies fresh air.

LEFT: Manual and electromagnetic locks were fitted to all doors.

BELOW LEFT: The spare wheel is stored behind the windowless rear hatch; this one has never seen use and the original paint in the wheel nut wells is still pristine.

BELOW UPPER: Additional security mountings for the windscreen make it harder to remove.

BELOW LOWER: The steel lining inside is covered with electrostatic flocking.

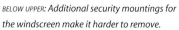

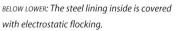

BELOW: A partition, with armoured door, separates the cab and load areas. The door can be operated only from the cab and an intercom provides communication.

BELOW: New large mirrors are mounted on reinforced brackets.

GLASS DELIVERY

As seen elsewhere, glass delivery conversions were used from 1951. The German company Hegla, based in Beverungen, specialized in Glass Transport vehicles; their brochure from the 1980s shows both T2 and T3 versions on Pick-Up and Panel Van bases.

LEFT AND BELOW: These Panel Van T4s with special glass carrying frames were also Hegla conversions. Note the additional wide load warning lights at bumper height in front of each wheel arch.

BUNDESPOST VEHICLES

The German Post Office made extensive use of the VW Bus for its delivery and support services. The Bundespost High Roof version was used for parcel delivery and often featured a driver's swivel front seat and a special sliding rack to load parcels through the rear tailgate, as well as being kitted out with shelving. In 1965 two prototype test vehicles were built specially for the Bundespost, though neither went into production due to costs. One featured a roof height sliding door, which Volkswagen was not convinced was stable enough, the other featured a smaller half High Roof built by Westfalia.

Yellow liveried vehicles were used for letters and parcels, while the grey-green versions were for radio/telephone services. Panel Vans, Kombis and Pick-Ups were all used.

RIGHT: *This 1951 example of a liveried Bundespost Van was shown in a 1952 sales brochure. Note the full-length roof rack bolted directly onto the roof and step mounted on the body side.*

ABOVE: *Two prototype Bundespost vehicles, one featuring a full-height sliding door and one with a smaller high roof and standard sliding door were built in 1965.*

BELOW: *Both vehicles carry the WOB plate used on test vehicles. Production costs proved too expensive and the vehicles never saw service.*

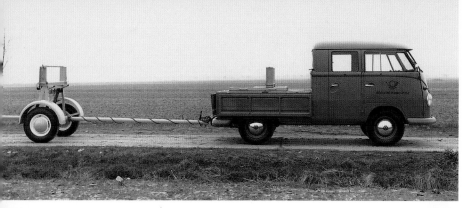

LEFT: The SO 14 trailer set up was ideal for carrying telegraph poles.

BELOW: This T3 Telekom Doka has the SO 24 style pole-carrying box trailer set up.

SWISS POSTAL VANS

The Swiss postal service also made use of High Roof Delivery Vans featuring a full-height sliding door. The Swiss importer AMAG imported special order walk-through RHD Panel Vans which were closed both sides, with no side door openings. Between 1962 and 1966 they produced a Delivery Van using this base specifically for the Swiss postal service. It featured a narrower, full-height sliding door, and the interior was fitted out for postal delivery. The door mechanisms were supplied by Wegmann of Bettenhausen, Germany, and the conversion was carried out by Gangloff of Bern, a company that specialized in building cable cars. The parts and conversion work increased the cost of these buses by twenty-five per cent of the cost of the basic bus.

The new full-height sliding door and guide rail can be seen on this Swiss Postal Van, currently being restored. The original seam from the cargo door opening and the new full-height half panel are clearly visible.

Many commercial vehicles have been saved by converting to Campers, as in this Swiss Postal Van.

THE FRIDOLIN

Although, strictly speaking, the Type 147 Post Delivery Van, often known as the Fridolin, is not a special bodied bus, it was a special model built in the Westfalia factory and known as Sonderfahrzeug Post. Developed specially for the German postal services during 1962/63, it also was used as a fleet vehicle by Lufthansa. Using a Karmann Ghia chassis, and Type 1 (Beetles), Type 3 (Notchbacks) and Type 2 (VW Bus) parts, it featured twin sliding doors and an opening tailgate. Type 2 influences can especially be seen at the rear end, which features a T1 engine lid, pre-1963-style small tailgate, the T1 oval rear light cluster, and the T1 rear bumper, which had to be cut down to fit and then re-welded. The Fridolin went into production in February 1964 and, by the end of production in 1973, 6,139 vehicles had been produced, with eighty-five per cent of these going to the Bundespost. Volkswagen also marketed the Fridolin to small businesses as the Kleinlieferwagen (small delivery van).

ABOVE: SO 16 brochure picture.

BELOW: 1953 Brochure introducing the Binz Double Cab model.

One of the first special body conversions of what would later become an official SO model and, subsequently, a Volkswagen model in its own right,

was the Double Cab Pick-Up built by the Binz Karosseriefabrik. Initially listed as M16 (Pick with Double Cab), with the introduction of the new SO designations and listings in 1957 it then became SO 16. This new SO (Sonderausführung, or Special Model) designation covered models that required additional special technical specifications or equipment and body or chassis

modifications as well as specific option packages. Double Cab conversions are commonly known as Doka, an abbreviation from the German word 'Doppelkabine' (literally Double Cab).

The Binz Karosseriefabrik, based in Lorch, Württemberg, which was already widely known for its coachbuilt conversions, introduced its version of a Double Cab in October 1953.

LORCHER KAROSSERIEFABRIK

BINZ & Co

LORCH (WÜRTT.)

ZOLLSTRASSE 2

TELEFON: LORCH (WÜRTT.) 416, 485

Lorch Württ. im Oktober 1953

Beschreibung und Preisliste 10 53 für VW-Doppelkabinen-Fahrerhaus

1

Preis des grundierten VW-Pritschenwagens   DM 6050.-

2

Anbau einer Kabine an das Fahrerhaus. Diese ist in der äußeren Form der VW-Linie angeglichen. Die Rückwand wird hierzu ca. 950 mm nach hinten versetzt. Die Kabine hat auf der rechten Seite in Fahrtrichtung eine Türe, die mit einem festeingebauten Fenster versehen ist. Die Türbreite beträgt ca. 800 mm. Die Kabinentür sowie die gegenüberliegende Seite ist innen mit Hartfaserplatte ausgeschlagen. Das linke Fenster in der Kabine ist als Schiebefenster ausgeführt. Hinter der vorderen Sitzbank befindet sich eine bis Höhe Rückenlehne durchgehend gesickte Blechwand. Die Pritsche und die Pritschenlänge sind um ca. 950 mm gekürzt. Sämtliche neuen und geänderten Teile sind grundiert: DM 895.-

3

Eine herausnehmbare Rohrgestell-Sitzbank kann zusätzlich auf besonderen Wunsch geliefert werden. Die Kabine kann dadurch nicht nur als Laderaum, sondern auch als Fahrgastraum Verwendung finden. Die Sitzbank ist mit Texleder im Farbton des Fahrersitzes bezogen. Sie hat eine Schlingfederkerneinlage und ist elastisch gepolstert. Die Befestigungsteile und die Bodenverstärkung werden mitgeliefert bzw. montiert: DM 166.-

4

Kompl. Lackierung in Kunstharz-Emaille, einfarbig   DM 185.- (Farbe nach Wunsch)

Nach dem Umbau beträgt das Steuergewicht ca. 950 kg. Die Preise verstehen sich bei frachtfreier Anlieferung des VW-Pritschenwagens an unser Werk Lorch Württ. Die Lieferung erfolgt frei Werk Lorch/Württ.

Lieferzeit: Nach Vereinbarung.

Zahlung: Die Bezahlung des Umbaus erfolgt in bar.
In besonderen Fällen kann eine andere Zahlungsweise vereinbart werden.

Im übrigen gelten unsere allgemeinen Lieferbedingungen vom 15. 9. 51 .

Apparently the owner of a Garden Nursery had visited the Binz factory and asked if they could create a version of the new VW Pick-Up Single Cab that would be able to transport plants and materials but would also offer a protected space for sensitive plants and for carrying workers to and from site. The result was the Binz Doka.

Volkswagen supplied Single Cabs in primer to the Binz factory, where the rear section of the cab was cut off and moved back 85cm. A roof section, side door and bulkhead panel were then installed to create the rear cab area, using lead filling for seams and joins. The side gates were then cut and welded to fit the smaller flatbed load area. Most Binz Dokas were finished in a version of Dove Blue, and workmanship was not always of a high standard, with visible weld seams on the side gates, the ashtray left in when the dash was painted and the engine compartment left in primer! Distinctive Binz features include the original bed seam still visible on the left side, non-opening large rear cab windows, tubular frame rear seat and 'suicide style' opening crew door. (Note, however, the few produced after the introduction of Volkswagen's Type 26 had a traditional forward opening door like Volkswagen's version.) Each vehicle also carried a Binz maker's plate showing its unique production number. These ID numbers are all pre-fixed 3635, the meaning of which is currently unknown.

Only around 550 Binz Dokas were actually produced (with many being exported to the USA) and production ceased in February 1959, as Volkswagen had introduced their own factory version (Type 265) the previous November. Very few of the original Binz conversions still survive, with just a handful still on the road today.

This works photograph dates from 1957. Note the rear hinged new cab door with sealed window, and the cut-down side gate with one moulding shorter than the others. Later VW Dokas had three equal size mouldings.

The Binz was especially popular with municipal work gangs.

Though ultra rare in Europe, US shows are occasionally graced by an unrestored, original condition Binz.

Binz installed a new bulkhead panel between the original and new cab areas.

BINZ 3635-187

This Binz was built in May 1958, serial number 3635-187, and, like many Binz conversions, was then exported to the USA. It was fully restored by Dan Kinsey in 2002, and is now powered by a 1776cc motor coupled to Rancho transmission. Other modifications include a 1966 front beam and upgraded brakes. Safari windows and rare Harp Arm large wing mirrors add custom detailing to an otherwise stock-looking bus.

A very distinctive Binz feature is the 'suicide' rear door that opens into oncoming traffic. Note also the fixed window and tubular frame rear seat.

BINZ 3635-174

Also built in May 1958, on serial number 3635-174, and exported to the USA, this Binz Doka eventually ended up being used as a mobile burger bar in Florida and was a hurricane victim before being imported to the UK in a very sorry state. It has had a full restoration by Rick Rowarth and Matt Smith, and was faithfully rebuilt using NOS parts and panels wherever possible. This included sourcing a Binz tubular seat frame in Germany, NOS side gates which had to be cut and then re-welded leaving the weld seams visible as Binz did, re-skinning the Binz rear cab door and getting it to fit properly, and completely re-leading all the cab section. It was then fitted with a genuine 1958 Okrasa engine. After attending Bad Camberg in 2007 it was sold on to an Austrian collector and is the only known roadworthy Binz in Europe.

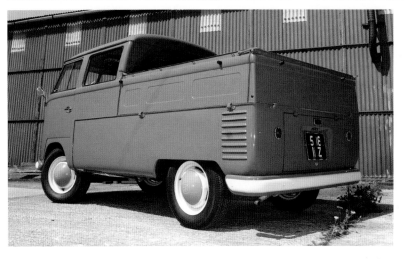

The original load bed seam is clearly visible showing where the new cab section was created.

To create the extra space Binz cut off the rear section of the cab and moved it back 85cm. A roof section, side door and bulkhead panel were then installed to make the rear cab area.

RIGHT: The side gates were cut and welded to fit the smaller flatbed load area and the resulting weld seams were left visible.

LEFT: The tubular frame rear seat was fabricated by Binz and is a notoriously hard part to find!

KRANKEN-TRANSPORTER

3

ambulance conversions (Type 27)

Within six months of the start of Transporter production, the Miesen Karosseriewerk, based in Bonn and which specialized in medical equipment and Ambulance conversions, had introduced a fully kitted out Ambulance, complete with stretcher and removable folding chair. The height of the Barndoor engine compartment meant rear access was impractical, so the loading and unloading of stretchers was via the cargo doors using a pivoting frame. Access was helped by provision of a slide-out step. Two fold-down jump seats were fitted to the bulkhead, and there were three standard layout options, depending on how many nurses were carried. Side windows were partially frosted and an illuminated Red Cross sign was mounted on the cab roof with two fresh air roof vents fitted above the load area. The

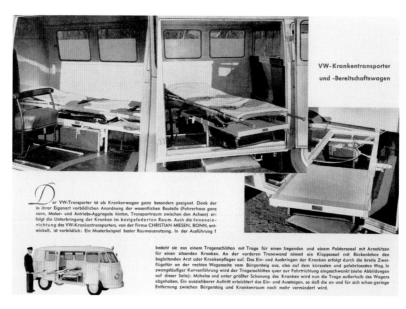

VW-Krankentransporter
und -Bereitschaftswagen

Der VW-Transporter ist als Krankenwagen ganz besonders geeignet. Dank der in ihrer Eigenart vorbildlichen Anordnung der wesentlichen Bauteile (Fahrerhaus ganz vorn, Motor- und Antriebs-Aggregate hinten, Transportraum zwischen den Achsen) erfolgt die Unterbringung der Kranken im bestgefederten Raum. Auch die Inneneinrichtung des VW-Krankentransporters, von der Firma CHRISTIAN MIESEN, BONN, entwickelt, ist vorbildlich: Ein Musterbeispiel bester Raumausnutzung. In der Ausführung 1 besteht sie aus einem Tragenschlitten mit Trage für einen liegenden und einem Polstersessel mit Armstützen für einen sitzenden Kranken. An der vorderen Trennwand nimmt ein Klappsessel mit Rückenlehne den begleitenden Arzt oder Krankenpfleger auf. Das Ein- und Ausbringen der Kranken erfolgt durch die breite Zweiflügeltür an der rechten Wagenseite vom Bürgersteig aus, also auf dem kürzesten und gefahrlosesten Weg. In zwangsläufiger Kurvenführung wird der Tragenschlitten quer zur Fahrtrichtung eingeschwenkt (siehe Abbildungen auf dieser Seite). Mühelos und unter größter Schonung des Kranken wird nun die Trage außerhalb des Wagens abgehoben. Ein ausziehbarer Auftritt erleichtert das Ein- und Aussteigen, so daß die an und für sich schon geringe Entfernung zwischen Bürgersteig und Krankenraum noch mehr vermindert wird.

The Kombi-based Ambulance conversion by the firm Miesen-Bonn was introduced in October 1950 and retained the large 'Barndoor' tailgate with a storage cupboard built over the engine, which was accessed from the rear via a small hatch. Stretchers were loaded via the cargo doors using a pivoting frame.

area above the engine compartment was boxed in and accessed by two doors from inside, while an opening rear hatch gave access from outside.

Volkswagen had planned an Ambulance version of the Transporter from the early development days in 1949, and the first VW Type 27, the new model code for the Krankenwagen, rolled off the production line on 13 December 1951 (#20 019 498). Volkswagen worked closely with the German Ambulance service and the Red Cross to develop a new model with a more flexible access than the Miesen version. This resulted in a radical redesign at the rear. In order to accommodate stretcher access via the rear, a large opening tailgate, lowered engine compartment shelf and smaller engine tailgate were created. (Interestingly, these changes became standard for all models as part of the 1955 post Barndoor bus specification.) The smaller engine lid also meant the fuel filler had to be sited externally at the rear side and was now accessed by a small D-shaped flap. Miesen influences can be seen in the provision of a sliding step and folding jump seat on the bulkhead. The initial factory versions had the new tailgate hinged at the top but, in response to feedback, within a few months a new reinforced tailgate that was hinged at the bottom and supported by chains was fitted. (From March 1963 the chains were replaced by hinged supports.) This gave an additional supporting platform for loading and unloading stretchers. Protective bars were fitted to frosted side windows and an electric rotary fresh air fan fitted in the roof. From January 1954 the Behr air scoop was also fitted as standard until the introduction of the revised Transporter in March 1955.

The Krankenwagen model also benefited from improvements long before they became standard equipment for all models. For example, a fuel gauge was standard from April 1954 and screen washers from October 1959. The standard Ambulance colour was Ivory White (RAL 1014) with black or grey upholstery/interior trim. The wheels were Lotus White, and the bumpers Ivory. Early Red Cross Ambulances were often painted Grey, the traditional German Red Cross colour for vehicles.

The new VW Ambulance was introduced in December 1951, with top hinged opening tailgate and small engine lid, as seen in this article featuring the factory prototype.

The 1951 brochure had to be changed as within a few months the tailgate was now hinged at the bottom. The early version featured a fold-out support deck, supported by struts.

Early Red Cross Ambulances were often painted Grey, the traditional German Red Cross colour for vehicles.

This January 1957 Ambulance is fully original and complete.

1957 AMBULANCE

This original condition version, finished in the standard Ivory White L62, rolled of the production line in January 1957 on chassis number 224 501 and carried the standard Ambulance package and fittings. In order to provide support for loading stretchers, tailgates for Ambulances were much heavier and hinged at the bottom. Standard equipment included a slide-out side step, tow hooks, reversing light, a sliding glass partition between the cab and load bay, three-quarter frosted glass and protective bars for side windows, blue flashing light and illuminated sign over the cab roof. The interior was trimmed in washable cream plastic, with rubber lower sections on the load doors for added protection. Inside was room for two stretchers, a folding jump seat against the bulkhead, a removable single seat and a slide-out single seat with armrests, as well as shelving and storage spaces for surgical equipment and instruments.

It was acquired in fully equipped, original condition by Michael Zierz in 1986; since then he has maintained its original condition and, accompanied by Nurse Anna in a period uniform, the bus is often displayed at special events, where they always draw a crowd of admirers! Still with its original 1200cc engine and with just 30,000 kilometres (19,000 miles) on the clock it is another piece of history preserved.

The interior still has its original equipment and fittings right down to the folding stretcher with leather securing straps and gas mask.

STANDARD AMBULANCE EQUIPMENT

- Illuminated sign on roof
- Searchlight
- Reversing light
- Folding platform for carrying stretchers
- Sliding step under the side doors with automatic safety mechanism
- Stretchers (two), mattresses, pillows
- Grab handles next to stretchers
- Buzzer for signalling the driver
- Rails and mounts for sliding and clamping stretchers

The illuminated Red Cross symbol has been replaced with a Bulli Kartei badge as the Ambulance is no longer in service.

The strengthened engine lid folds down to act as support for loading the stretcher.

The large tailgate is hinged at the bottom. Note period details like small rear lights and engine lid mounted brake light, reversing light, tow hook and pressed bumpers.

BELOW: An additional, removable single seat is secured by floor clamps while the other single seat with armrests is on runners allowing it to be slid in and out of place.

A folding jump seat is mounted on the bulkhead and a sliding glass partition separates the driver from the rear area.

Wipe-clean plastic covers all interior panels and the side windows are partially frosted with protective bars. Load doors also have rubber protection on the lower sections.

A slide-out step was standard for all Ambulances.

It was possible to lay out the interior to carry two stretchers and a nurse.

In order to provide support for loading stretchers, tailgates for Ambulances were much heavier and hinged at the bottom. An extension flap was available as an option.

- Upholstered patient chair with armrests
- Upholstered seat with folding back
- Folding seat on bulkhead
- Linoleum covering for floor and platform
- Interior panelling in washable cream-coloured plastic
- Cabinet and drawer for utensils, instruments and general storage
- Extra storage area
- Shelf for splints
- Opening windows (two) in the rear bay
- Three-quarter frosted glass in the rear bay
- Window bars on all rear windows except forward side door window
- Sliding window and roll-up blind between rear bay and driver's cab
- Dimmer switch for rear bay lighting (operated from driver's cab)
- Heating in rear bay, electrical fresh air fans in the cab roof
- Fuel gauge and reserve lever
- Electric sockets for hand torches
- Grab handle on driver's cabin wall.

Volkswagen's basic Type 27 Ambulance met all the technical specifications for every emergency service and was used not only by health authorities and hospital accident services but was also often attached to fire stations and rescue units. They were also used extensively in the private sector in places such as clinics, retirement homes, hospices and factories. Some of these uses required special equipment, and various grouped options had a specific M code. For example, M150 was a special equipment package of tow hooks front and rear, opening window with bars on the forward side door, longer rails for ISO or American-type stretchers, hooks for intravenous bottles, holders for first aid kits, spades and axes and an electric socket for hand-held torches. Other common Ambulance options included M28 (no stretcher), M151 (Eberspächer heater), M152 (tailgate extension panel), M160 (blue light and Bosch siren) and M623 (short-wave radio equipment).

Like the fire service vehicles, the Ambulance continued as a production model throughout Bay and T3 generations, seeing general use as well as specialized use as mobile premature baby units and road accident/disaster vehicles. With the introduction of the T4 generation however, Volkswagen decided to no longer make a factory Ambulance, instead outsourcing and providing base models to Volkswagen-approved firms like Miesen, which produced the first VW Ambulance back in October 1950.

SPECIAL EQUIPMENT SO 29 AND SO 30

Though not special body models, two specialized Ambulance equipment models also had SO designations. SO 29 was a Catastrophe Trailer, while SO 30 was a Drag Sled designed to get injured miners out of very narrow tunnels and called the Gruben-schleifkorb (literally mine slip basket or Drag Sled).

Miesen still equip VW-based Ambulances, as in this T4 version.

A fuel gauge was standard on all Ambulances from April 1954.

Standard equipment included an illuminated roof light with a Red Cross or the logo of the organization; this example is the ASB (Workers' Samaritan Federation) logo of a red 'S' on a yellow cross.

SO 29 CATASTROPHE TRAILER

To increase the flexibility of the emergency services, a specialized trailer for use with the VW Ambulance was offered by Hahn Fahrzeugbau of Stuttgart. Available from 1952, as can be seen in the period publicity photograph, it was designed specifically for use in attending road accidents, and equipment such as torches, tools and road signs was carried as well as additional medical supplies. Paired with an Ambulance, this provided necessary additional equipment, all neatly labelled, boxed and bagged, so that a mobile field unit could be set up at the scene of the accident/disaster. The trailer had wood sides with a hinged hardtop cover, and was painted Ivory; Red Cross insignia was optional. Note also the full-length roof rack fitted to the partner Ambulance shown here. When towing the maximum permitted speed was 40km/h (25mph), and Volkswagen approved the increased towing weight from 500kg to 750kg.

From 1959 the Hahn Catastrophe Trailer was designated as SO 29.

RIGHT: It was fully equipped with additional medical supplies, torches, tools, road signs etc, boxed and bagged, and ready to set up a mobile field unit.

This 1952 factory picture shows an early Ambulance (note the D-shaped fuel flap) with full-length roof rack and cover and SO 29 Hahn trailer.

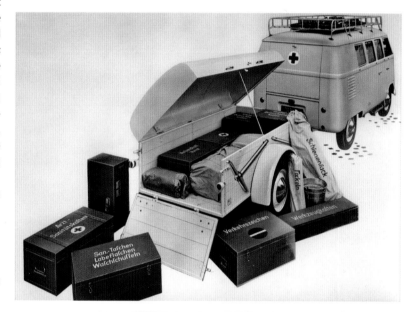

ABOVE AND BELOW: Designed specifically for use in mines and confined spaces, the Grubenschleifkorb, manufactured by UTILA-Gerätebau Werner Geyr, was listed in dealership optional equipment catalogues from 1958 as SO 30. It was a metal-framed 'stretcher', with fold-down metal side protection panels and steel runners. It could be dragged or pushed. Handles could be attached for carrying.

The SO 29 trailer had wood sides and a hard top. The tow bar was extendable.

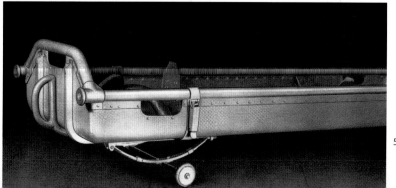

RIVER RESCUE AMBULANCES

Areas near to rivers often had dedicated River Rescue vehicles, usually crewed and operated by volunteers.

RIGHT: 1956 Wolfsburg River Rescue. A pole-mounted emergency spotlight, mirror stalk searchlight and inflatable dinghy form part of the equipment of this River Rescue Ambulance, used by the Wolfsburg Town Council.

LEFT: 1957 Karlsruhe Fire Department Ambulance. Equipped specifically to deal with emergencies on the River Rhien, which flows near the city, this 1957 Ambulance has been finished in Fire Truck Red and distinctive black detailing on body bumpers and wheels. As well as a fibreglass boat, the roof rack also carries boat hooks and grab poles and folding ladders for use on ice. It has been updated with a flashing blue light, bullet indicators and after market twin siren.

CENTRE LEFT: 1976 River Lifeguard Service. This 1976 Ambulance tows a power boat for patrolling and watching over swimmers and was used in the east Bavaria region.

BELOW LEFT: 1969 DLRG Rescue Service. DLRG is the German Life Saving Society, which used Ambulances to supervise and rescue swimmers. This 1969 example was used on the River Main around Frankfurt and has the Society's logo on the front.

BELOW RIGHT: This T3 example of a DLRG Rescue Ambulance was also used in the Frankfurt area. The half-frosted side windows show it to be a full Ambulance conversion. Note the bank of four sirens on the front and the loudspeaker on the roof between the blue lights.

CLINOMOBIL HIGH ROOF AMBULANCE

In 1963 the firm Clinomobil, based in Hanover, produced an Ambulance conversion, based on a factory High Roof model; the extra space inside enabled more equipment to be carried with the added bonus that nurses and health workers could stand up inside. Early versions had two windows on each side, and a single rear flap, but the later versions from 1966 featured three windows on each side and an additional opening flap at the rear above the tailgate. Additional warning flashers were also mounted at the rear of the roof.

BELOW LEFT: This early 1963 Clinomobil would have been one of the first produced and was used by the German Red Cross.

BELOW RIGHT: Until 1966 the Clinomobil had two windows in each side and just a standard tailgate at the rear.

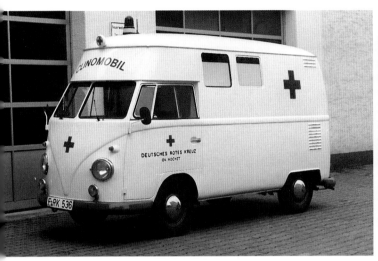

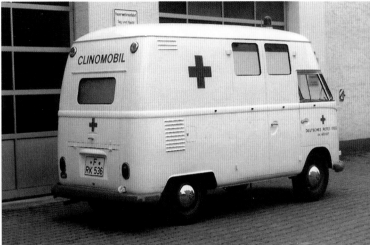

1967 JOHANNITER CLINOMOBIL

LEFT: This 1967 Clinomobil was used by the Johanniter Humanitarian Organization, formed originally from crusading medieval knights, as evidenced by the Maltese Cross symbol. Note the special side mirror arms and convoy flag mounting point.

RIGHT: The increased space and headroom offered by the Clinomobil was especially welcomed by health workers.

LEFT: From 1966 an additional rear opening section in the roof above the tailgate made for better access.

RIGHT: Later Clinomobils also featured three windows in each side.

Westfalia's High Roof Ambulance was introduced in 1963. Based on a Panel Van, the rear and sides were cut off and a new coachbuilt box section grafted on behind the cab.

WESTFALIA HIGH ROOF AMBULANCE

From 1963 to 1966 Westfalia produced their own version of a High Roof Ambulance, to compete with the Clinomobil. Using a basic Panel Van, the rear and sides were cut off and a new coachbuilt box section grafted on behind the cab. Side panels were corrugated for stiffness and strength and a single partly frosted window fitted on each side with stretcher access via twin rear doors. Each was hand built to order and slightly different but, as they were expensive to produce and the Clinomobil proved more popular, very few were actually built.

The version pictured here was built in December 1963 and left the factory as a Panel Van with factory-fitted options of 1500cc engine/1 ton payload (M215), 12V electrics (M620), short-wave radio equipment (M623), tow hooks (M029), steering/ignition lock (M056) and Eberspächer heater (M119). Originally painted in Ivory White, it was used by a private hospital and then a municipal authority for transport, when it was repainted in the standard Orange used for public service vehicles.

ABOVE: Side panels were corrugated for stiffness and strength and a single partly frosted window fitted on each side with stretcher access via twin rear doors.

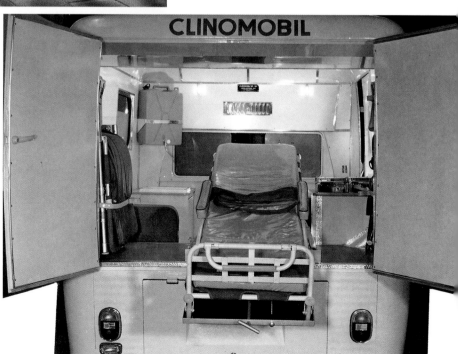

RIGHT: Factory photograph showing the interior fitments on the Westfalia Ambulance.

HILFS-KRANKENWAGEN (AUXILIARY AMBULANCE)

Some Ambulances used by voluntary services such as the Red Cross or ASB (Workers' Samaritan Federation) were kitted out as Mannschafts-Transportwagen (personnel transport), carrying doctors, paramedics and portable emergency medical equipment to scenes of major accidents and disasters. Also known as Hilfs-Krankenwagen (literally help ambulance) they were not fully converted specialist Ambulances and featured two bench seats and clear side windows. However, a special split rear seat arrangement meant part or all could be folded down to allow patients on stretchers to be carried. When not in use the stretchers folded and were stored behind the seat in the luggage area. They were also fitted with convoy flag mountings and external battery-charging sockets.

This 1978 T2 was used for personnel transport, but could also double as an Ambulance ferrying stretcher patients.

RIGHT: A special split rear seat arrangement meant part, or all, could be folded down to allow patients on stretchers to be carried.

RIGHT: The bulkhead bench seat was the rear folding split seat installed the other way round to make a base for stretchers.

ambulance conversions (Type 27)

AMBULANCE GALLERY

RIGHT: 1971 standard Krankenwagen.

BELOW LEFT: Later style Bay Type 27 Ambulance, used by the German Red Cross. Note the red-painted front grill.

BELOW RIGHT: Several organizations used Ambulances, such as this version used by the Johanniter Humanitarian Society featuring their distinctive Maltese Cross logo and livery.

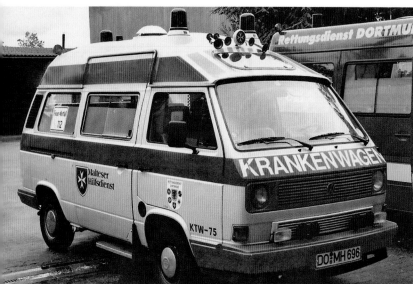

ABOVE LEFT: This odd photograph shows a married couple still in their wedding attire being shown a premature baby unit!

ABOVE RIGHT: This Ambulance is kitted out with a premature baby unit complete with incubators. The chrome trim and bumpers show it was originally a Deluxe Microbus.

LEFT: This Dehler body conversion has a distinctive Dehler roof with mouldings for emergency lights and door height extension and Carat-style bumpers.

ABOVE LEFT: *This is a Syncro 4WD High Roof model. Note the higher sliding door, window in the roof front and rear-facing spotlight.*

ABOVE RIGHT: *This T3 ELW unit acted as a command and coordination vehicle in major emergencies, and was used by the Munich Fire Department.*

RIGHT: *This publicity shot of the new T4 Ambulance conversion, complete with rolling stretcher assembly, uses the same backdrop and action pose as an original 1960 version.*

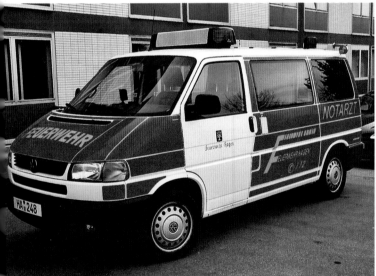

ABOVE LEFT: *As part of a move to an integrated emergency service, the Notarzt T4 is a command vehicle run by a doctor who coordinates a team of paramedics.*

ABOVE RIGHT: *Paramedics operate from fully equipped Emergency vehicles such as this one, coordinated by the Fire Department.*

RIGHT: *The T5 has seamlessly carried on the VW Ambulance heritage. This conversion is by Systemtechnik.*

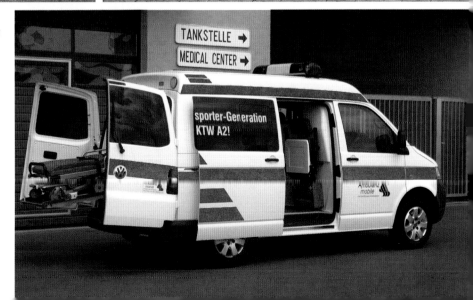

broadcasting, film projection and radio buses

ABOVE: *Other 1951/52 liveried broadcasting buses included one used by Philips in Holland with a TV aerial and a ladder and roof platform to position the aerial and monitor signal strength.*

This image of a Loudspeaker Van appeared in the 1952 Who Drives a VW Transporter? brochure.

The first use of a VW Transporter for radio and amplified sound broadcasting was described in the November 1951 *VW Information*, and the 1955 *Special Interiors* brochure showed two very early (pre-1952) versions. One featured a large antenna, which was mounted on the floor of the cargo area and extended up through the roof, and the other was a film projection bus. The latter was built on an Ambulance base as the small engine lid allowed for a projection screen to be sited in the large opening for the tailgate. A fold-out shield cut down on light interference, and both moving and still images were back projected onto the screen from inside the van.

Various forms of broadcast and projection buses were also used by the police and fire services for educational purposes.

RIGHT: This 1951 Kombi was fitted with roof-mounted loudspeakers and a TV aerial to demonstrate radios and TV sets, which were set up inside.

BELOW LEFT: : An image from the 1955 Special Interiors brochure shows a 1951 Microbus used as a Funkmesswagen to trace radio interference, with a huge radio transmission aerial. Note the blackout facilities for the windows.

BELOW RIGHT: Also shown in the brochure was a very early example of a film projection unit with the screen mounted in, and viewed from, the rear. To allow the fitting of this, an Ambulance model with a small engine lid was used (note also the Ambulance model's side window protection bars).

LEFT AND BELOW: These images, printed in the 1962 VW Commercials Equipped for Many Purposes brochure, show a variety of broadcasting and radio uses including a TV Detector Van, the Ambulance-based film projection car interior shot used in the 1955 brochure, and various interior configurations fitted with reel to reel tape and vinyl record deck equipment

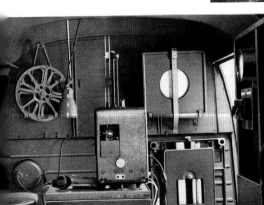

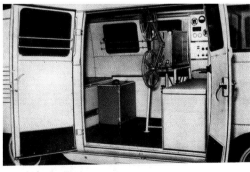

1955 MOBILE RADIO STATION WZLS BUS

In 1956 North Carolina based Radio WZLS (with its 'The Home of Rock 'n' Roll' slogan) kitted out a 1955 Deluxe Microbus as a mobile recording and broadcasting studio, complete with record decks. Finished in the company colours of navy blue/silver grey and signwriting, it also featured chromed bumpers and a side step. A large aerial was originally mounted on the rear roof section. The bus is now part of the Grundmann's Museum collection, and a Wiking model of it was made especially for the Hessisch Oldendorf Show in 2009. Parked in the main square, it was used as the Event HQ for live announcements and music.

ABOVE LEFT: Curving workspace allows for a variety of recording and playback equipment to be easily accessed by the disc jockey.

ABOVE RIGHT: All the original broadcasting and recording equipment is still intact and functioning such as the twin record decks and mixer. The modern PA equipment was added for the old-timer show in Hessisch.

LEFT: The Radio WZLS bus in use at Hessisch Oldendorf in 2009.

1966 FILMWAGEN

'The Cinecar is a mobile cinema exclusively designed for serving all features of modern information and advertisement dissemination' is how Cinecar Productions of Bonn described their high-roof mobile film wagon. It followed the same basic principles as the pre-1952 version but being a High Roof model meant the rear projection screen was much larger, as was the fold-out light shield. Speakers were mounted in the rear load area, hidden behind a cut-out panel just above the engine lid and in the front above the front windscreens. Power was supplied by the engine-driven dynamo or a special battery unit and the Cinecar was used for taped announcements as well as film projection. The high roof meant full-scale modern film projection equipment fitted in easily and there was also more room for the projectionist. The version shown here is the only one known to still exist in its original condition. It is now in the private collection of Charlie Hamill in California.

ABOVE: Extra speakers were mounted in the High Roof model's front.

RIGHT: The high roof was perfect for both 16mm film projection and the projectionist.

BELOW: A large projection screen with fold-out light shield was sited on the rear deck, with speakers below it.

The telecommunications side of Deutsche Bundespost used a specially equipped radar van, known as a Funkmesswagen or sometimes as a Peilwagen (literally locating van), whose job was to look for sources of radio interference and monitor signal strength. The version pictured here was a twin sliding door Kombi built in 1976 and features a twin antenna set up. A single swivel seat faces the bank of screens and gauges in the rear, housed over an office-style desk. It now resides in the Communications Museum, Frankfurt.

ABOVE: *The Funkmesswagen was designed to look for sources of radio interference and monitor signal strength.*

LEFT: *It was based on a double door Kombi for flexible access.*

RIGHT: *Two large aerials were mounted on the roof.*

LEFT: *A single swivel seat faces the bank of screens and gauges in the rear, housed over an office-style desk.*

In late 1952 the salt mine near Northeim, Germany, converted two VW Transporters to be used for ferrying miners and equipment and towing carts in the tunnels of the salt mines, approximately six hundred and sixty-five metres underground. As can be seen, the vehicles were a strange hybrid of Panel Van and VW Ambulance chassis, with no side windows and a large tailgate/small engine lid. The tailgate, cargo doors and cab doors were all removed to make for easy access and a reinforced towing bar and standing plate welded at the rear. An extra side opening was cut into the driver's side in much the same way as the twin cargo door option for Panel Vans, giving access for workers on both sides. The front screens were retained but the wiper assembly removed. Exhaust fumes were extracted by means of ventilation ducts and pipes sited in the roofs of the tunnels.

tank track Bullis

ABOVE: *1962 Prototype all-terrain half-track Raupen Fuchs conversion.*

RAUPEN FUCHS

During the 1960s there were several attempts in Austria to convert a Bulli to run on tank tracks. Presumably the Alpine conditions and terrain dictated a possible need for a vehicle able to cope with steep inclines, mud and snow. The vehicle shown here was a prototype built by Raupen Fuchs (literally Caterpillar Fox) and designed for use as an Alpine shuttle bus for transporting tourists to and from hotels and guest houses in winter conditions.

The Raupen Fuchs uses a May 1962 Kombi as the base vehicle (chassis 940 045) and features two steerable front wheels and a half-track set up for the twin rear wheels. It is fitted with a planetary gearbox on the rear axle and could reach speeds of 40km/h (25mph)! Weighing in at 1,300kg, it could carry seven passengers, with seating for six in the rear. However, despite its all-terrain ability it was actually very awkward and difficult to manoeuvre. The engine was not really powerful enough and there was also no real demand or need for such a vehicle as the Kässbohrer PistenBully snowmobiles were proven, purpose-built vehicles. Although a brochure extolling its ability to cope with 'sand and snow, forest and meadow' exists, none ever made it into production.

The model shown here was 'discovered' by Bulli Kartei enthusiasts in 1994, tucked away in the Porsche Museum in Gmünd, Austria and brought back to working order, attending shows like Bad Camberg in 1999. Since then it has been put back in storage by Bulli Kartei, awaiting restoration to its former glory one day.

Another prototype version, featuring a Kombi bodyshell fitted to a complete tank-style track set up, was built by workers for the German Bundespost around 1966 in the Nuremberg area. They needed a vehicle to access and service a TV mast, sited on a mountain. There is a 'home movie' film record, shot by a worker, of its very first test drive and approval by inspectors and then of the finalized version skidding around in snow at the works. It was fast and highly manoeuvrable and because it had no steering wheel, just two joysticks to control the amount of torque delivered to each drive train, controlling speed and direction was a bit hit and miss. It is not known what happened to this vehicle or if it actually saw service.

The side doors had to be cut down and a new full-length wheel/track protection shield fitted.

It was originally designed for use as an Alpine shuttle bus for transporting tourists in winter.

With two steerable front wheels, and a half track set up for the twin rear wheels, it can cope with difficult ground conditions.

Despite its all terrain set up, it was actually very tricky to drive and manoeuvre.

Fritz Punsch from Austria also tried out fitting tank tracks to a VW Bus, as can be seen in this example of a 1953 Kombi being put through its paces.

airport buses

ABOVE: *This 1966 Kombi in full Lufthansa livery is now part of Volkswagen's museum.*

The German airline Lufthansa was one of the first customers to use specially adapted Transporters as fleet vehicles and it commissioned two special body conversions in 1950/51. The Follow Me Buses were used to guide planes to and from the runway and terminal parking and one of these was described and shown in the November 1951 edition of *VW Information*. Based on a Kombi, it featured a sliding roof, Plexiglas cab sunroof and an additional window on each side to allow maximum visibility for ground crew. There was also another wider window in the rear, much wider than the optional Volkswagen version. An illuminated Follow Me sign (English

This Follow Me model was first described in November 1951 dealership information and shown here in a 1955 brochure. It featured a sliding roof, Plexiglas cab sunroof, rear window and additional windows on each side, with a large illuminated Follow Me sign.

This 1951 'hi-top' was used for ferrying aviation oil and fuel and featured a roof box for stowing a ladder and a side-hinged opening rear tailgate.

Another picture of the same 1951 refuelling van was used in the 1962 brochure showing a range of special purpose bodies.

being the universal language) faced rearwards on the roof and large circular rear lights with flashing arrows to show direction were also fitted, along with radio and communication equipment, storage for equipment and additional hand-held spotlights.

Another version, based on a Panel Van, was used for ferrying aviation oil and fuel. It featured a roof box for stowing a ladder and a side-hinged opening rear tailgate.

Painted in distinctive yellow and blue livery complete with the airline logo, Microbuses were also used by Lufthansa for personnel transport. By the 1960s Lufthansa-liveried buses had a variety of uses, from people, crew or baggage carriers to specialized conversion for pre-warming jet engines. Single and Double Cab Pick-Ups, Panel Vans and Microbuses were all used for various jobs. Larger airports also often had dedicated Fire and Emergency Trucks as part of the first response emergency teams. These varied uses continued through the Bay Window years, but by the 1980s the main use had become as crew or business passenger shuttles.

Many other airlines used liveried Microbuses for baggage and crew transport but none as extensively as Lufthansa. Military airbases also used Volkswagen versions of Follow Me Buses.

This collection of liveried buses used by Swiss Air and British European Airways appeared in the 1952 brochure Who Drives a VW Transporter?

LEFT: This 1951 Kombi has been used for the past thirty years or more on a gliding school field at Hornberg, near Stuttgart. A new owner and collector repainted it in the 1990s in the Lufthansa-style livery of blue and yellow, with a white roof. The cab doors carry the gliding school logo.

BELOW: This 1971 Bay Window pre-warmer, seen in use at Frankfurt airport, is based on a twin door Panel Van. A vented roof box provides cooling.

ABOVE: Dating from the late 1950s this archive shot shows a Single Cab converted for use in pre-warming jet engines prior to starting. The enclosed box on the load bed houses the pre-warming generator and has top hinged side access flaps on each side and mesh windows for cooling.

LEFT: This Ansett Air liveried Kombi was used by the Australian company as a personnel shuttle. The bus is a 1957/58 model and fitted with opening Safari front screens.

RIGHT: Trans Australia Airlines were also carriers for the Royal Mail. This 1957 Kombi was used for ferrying baggage and mail to and from the terminal.

BELOW LEFT: Airports often had their own dedicated Emergency vehicles, such as this 1972 Fire Truck based at Frankfurt. Note the large spotlight!

BELOW RIGHT: Lufthansa liveried fleet vehicles shown here include pre-warmers, Follow Me vehicles and mobile steps mounted on a Pick-Up base.

ABOVE: This specially adapted High Roof Bay was used for ferrying disabled passengers to and from the plane.

RIGHT: A 1971 early Bay in use as a Follow Me vehicle at Frankfurt airport.

T2 Personnel Transport; note the roof flashers.

This pre-1973 T2 Double Cab has received a new, later style, front panel at some point.

Top-of-the-range vehicles, like the LWB Multivan Business T4 shown here, are still used for Business Class and VIP passengers.

Publicity shot of the Amarok SUV used as an aviation fuel tow car exemplifies its multi-purpose usage.

RIGHT: T2 Kombis at Frankfurt airport.

9

SO 1 and SO 2 mobile shops

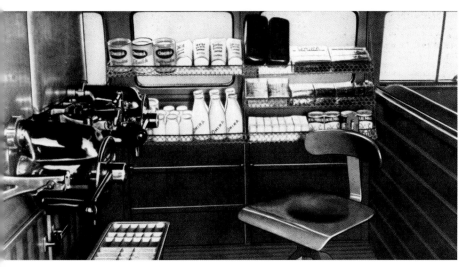

ABOVE: *This image of a mobile milk delivery van interior is more artist's impression than actual photograph, and was used in 1955 and 1962 publicity brochures.*

SO 1 MOBILE SHOP WITH SALES FLAP

Various conversions of Mobile Shops were shown in Volkswagen's in-house publication, *VW Information*, during 1951 and, by 1953, Westfalia was producing a Mobile Shop featuring a top hinged opening serving flap in the

BELOW LEFT: *The 1955 Special Interiors brochure carried these images of Mobile Shops based on 1951/52 Panel Vans, one with swing-out counter.*

BELOW RIGHT: *This 1951 milk delivery van (note long upper vents) had a sales flap and counter.*

Westfalia used walk-through models for SO 1 conversion; this works photo from 1959 shows a van ready to be kitted out.

Unusually this sales flap Mobile Shop also had cargo doors on the left side.

side, wood sales counter, and shelving/bin storage, which could be specified to the customer's own design. Usually, walk-through Panel Vans were used to allow access to the sales area from inside, freeing up one sidewall for shelving/display. Until 1967 there were also versions that retained cargo doors for access opposite the sales flap.

The fitted-out Westfalia Mobile Shop carried the SO 1 designation, but it was also possible to order an empty Panel Van with side-opening sales flap via Westfalia/Wiedenbrück directly from the Volkswagen factory dealer.

SO 1 featured a top hinged opening serving flap in the side, wood sales counter, and shelving/bin storage.

BELOW: In 1956 Volkswagen and Westfalia produced this famous mobile Post Office demonstration prototype for the Bundespost. As well as a sales counter, stamp machines and a post box were sited behind the tailgate. However, the Bundespost considered it too small and expensive and it never went into production.

SO 2 HIGH ROOF SALES VANS

Westfalia's SO 2 High Roof shop was kitted out similar to SO 1, with wood display counter. This factory shot dates from 1962.

With the introduction of the new factory large space Panel Van (Grossraum-Kastenwagen), commonly known as the High Roof model, in September 1961, businesses immediately took advantage of the increase in height. While the SO 1 conversion was popular, the new High Roof model was the preferred option when it became available because it was more comfortable for the shop assistant. As is the case with several Volkswagen models, such as the Crew Cab, the High Roof version grew from customer demand. Several Karosseriebau-Werke had carried out hi-top conversions (usually fibreglass) in the 1950s but, unlike these, the Volkswagen version, carrying the designation ID Type 21-222, had new full-size metal body panels and corners, including a special curved front panel above the windscreens. The upper cooling vents, fresh air intake and roof guttering were repositioned at the top of the bodyline, although the rain guttering around the front cab remained to help keep the windscreen clear. The guttering above the rear hatch also remained. Higher cargo doors were fitted, but not sliding doors because of instability. The increased space meant it was easy to fit shelving or rails and racks to hang goods and clothing from.

Westfalia were quick to capitalize on the new possibilities of the High Roof model, using the factory opening sales flap option for its SO 2 Mobile Shop conversion, (Grossraum-Verkaufswagen) with Volkswagen vehicle ID Type 21-221. Interior fittings were designed to suit individual customers, but the standard layout offered wooden display counter, circular stool and open shelving, cubby holes, drawers and cupboards.

This factory photograph of the same vehicle shows some well-dressed customers being served!

WESTFALIA
HIGH ROOF VARIANTS

Westfalia used only the High Roof option M221 (High Roof model with sales flap) for their Mobile Shop conversion (SO 2), which was based on a walk-through model (M80). However, Westfalia also used their own versions of a steel high roof, modelled on the Volkswagen option and grafted onto the standard Panel Van roof, for a series of Special Bodies, as can be seen in the Westfalia archive of factory photographs of prototypes and one-off orders.

ABOVE: 1960 Westfalia converted Panel Van. The special Westfalia High Roof has not yet had glass fitted to the long windows. Note the front safaris, original roof gutter and the Westy metal caravans in the background!

ABOVE: 1961 prototype with original roof gutter, smaller high roof, long roof windows, loading doors on the left and a small sales flap/counter. The photo was taken in Westfalia's private yard at the works in Wiedenbrück.

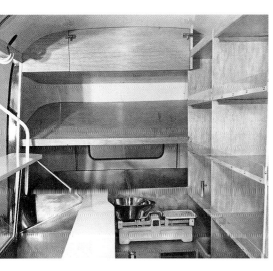

The interior of the fishmonger van was kitted out inside with wipe-clean surfaces, weighing scales and a fish storage tank under the counter.

1962 Volkswagen standard factory High Roof, with full-height cargo doors and sales flap (M221). This van was converted by Westfalia into a mobile fishmonger's.

1962 Westfalia High Roof model, equipped as a mobile bank and with cargo doors on the left. Fittings included 'bank office' furniture and a swivel seat for the driver/bank clerk. Note the original roof gutter and rear tailgate with no half moon recess or window.

1965 Westfalia Mobile Shop, based on the VW High Roof Bus. The sales flap has been placed where the cargo doors would have been. Note the gutter above the flap which protected customers from the rain. Only a handful of these were actually built.

Dortmunder Actien Bier sales van with removable sales flap.

Until 1967 Westfalia sales flap vehicles could have cargo doors on the left as well as a sales flap on the right, but from 1967 new German motoring regulations prohibited access doors on the left. One solution offered by Westfalia was to have a small half door access under the sales flap.

1963 SO 2 ICE CREAM VAN

The bus was ordered on 26 November 1963 and registered in Germany on 31 January 1964. It was supplied with windowless tailgate, and factory-fitted Ambulance fans and bumper over-riders, both of which it still has. It had originally been used as an Ice Cream Van (marks where the freezers were are still visible) and had at some point become a Camper.

In 2010 Daniel Dimbleby bought it, just beating the Volkswagen Museum! He had it fully restored, using NOS parts wherever possible, before repainting in VW Sea Green (a New Beetle colour) under Pearl White with the roof top also in Sea Green, a perfect colour combination for its rebirth as an Ice Cream Van once more.

Now fully kitted out with ice cream dispensers and freezers, it is signwritten with the name of Daniel's new business venture, the Split Screen Ice Cream Company, and debuted at shows and events in 2011.

This 1963 SO 2 was originally an Ice Cream Van and has just been fully restored for the Split Screen Ice Cream Company.

RIGHT: *Its sales flap offers all-weather protection for ice cream lovers.*

BELOW LEFT: *This was how the bus looked in 2010. US spec bumpers were factory fitted from new.*
BELOW RIGHT: *This version has the optional configuration of left hand high cargo doors opposite the sales hatch.*

SERVICE GARAGES CONVERSIONS

Service Garages was a specialist UK conversion company, which in 1963 produced several Special Bodies offering Mobile Shops and Refrigerated vehicles as well as a camping conversion. The Service Mobile Shop and the 'Serv-Ice' Ice Cream Van were based on walk-through Kombi models and were externally more or less identical, with a fixed fibreglass roof and windows on each side that gave in excess of six foot of headroom and a large sliding window and counter for sales. The Ice Cream Sales version was fully kitted out with ice cream dispenser and refrigerated storage as well as washing facilities. Options included fresh air fans, electronic chimes and signwriting or painting in company colours. The soft ice cream machine refrigerated cabinets and water heater were all driven by the vehicle's own power unit, dispensing with the need for subsidiary engine, generators, control gear and electric motors.

BELOW: The Ice Cream Sales version was fully kitted out with ice cream dispenser and refrigerated storage as well as washing facilities.

ABOVE: Servis conversions were based on walk-through Kombi models and were externally more or less identical, with a fixed fibreglass roof with windows on each side and a large sliding window.

BELGIAN MODELS

The Belgian company D'Ieteren produced a range of Special Bodies marketed as De Winkel Fleet. The range
included Mobile Shops, Taxis, Tippers,
Cherry Pickers, Emergency vehicles
and Campers. The brochure shown
here is for a Mobile Shop with a long
window in the high roof section above
the sliding door and sliding glass sales
window opposite.

*RIGHT: This 1963 sales High Roof was a special
body conversion by D'Ieteren, using their roof. It
was designed for use as an Ice Cream Van and
featured sliding sales windows on each side. It
surfaced in 1996 at VW Euro, where it was up
for sale.*

*BELOW: It was bought by a Dutch fast food
retailer and Volkswagen enthusiast, who
restored it, repainted it with the Stars and
Stripes livery and then used it as a Hot Dog Van,
even returning to VW Euro for several years.
Recently it was sold on and imported to the UK
where it still works at events and shows.*

BECK'S BEER VAN

This 1966 Panel Van has been fully restored and fitted out as a mobile pub complete with bar and draught beer. It is a regular attendee at major European shows and events and is pictured here at the Hanover 60 year celebrations and Hessisch Oldendorf 2009. It is now part of the Volkswagen Nutzfahrzeuge's Oldtimer Collection in Hanover.

T2 AND T3 MODELS

The Bay Window factory-fitted high roof option became available in January 1968, initially only for the Panel Van. Unlike the Split Screen model, this did not feature extended steel body panels but utilized a braced synthetic resin top, which was grafted onto the existing roof line after the original roof had been cut out. This had the added advantage of cutting costs, since new special size side panels or roof fronts did not have to be fabricated. M516 was the standard option, with a normal sized sliding door, but many of the High Roofers featured either the larger sliding door (M515) or the opening sales flap and counter arrangement, often converted by Westfalia. The high sliding door was especially popular with the German Post Office and also ice cream companies. In 1972 a high top version of the Kombi became available, and the option continued into production of the T3 and beyond.

This early Bay SO 1, seen here at a show in Switzerland, is now an unusual Camper.

RIGHT: Though no longer given an SO designation, Westfalia continued to offer Mobile Shop conversions as in this 1985 demonstration model.

RIGHT: This 1983 Karmann coachbuilt T3 version, on a Pick-Up base, features a large rear opening flap door as well as sales flap and counter.

LEFT: This air-cooled early 1980s High Roof T3 was converted in 2007 into a Hasseröder beer bar truck to serve the public at the 60th Anniversary International Volkswagen Bus Convention in Hanover. It was later given away in a raffle.

79

Originally used as a fire truck by a Swiss chemical company/factory, this 1964 Grossraum-Kastenwagen was fully restored in 2008/09 and turned into a mobile pub and bar, selling the famous Lauterbacher beer. The signwriting and logos are authentic copies of the original/historic brand signs used by Lauterbacher in the 1960s on their VW transporters, including the strapline, 'a delicious tradition'.

LEFT: The mobile sweetshop was a hit with children everywhere!

BELOW: The mobile shop tradition continues into the T5 generation. This coachbuilt version has a full-length opening flap offering all-weather protection for customers as well as a full-length sales counter.

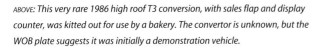

ABOVE: This very rare 1986 high roof T3 conversion, with sales flap and display counter, was kitted out for use by a bakery. The convertor is unknown, but the WOB plate suggests it was initially a demonstration vehicle.

RIGHT: These 1981 'Koffer' box vans, built on the air-cooled early T3 Panel Van chassis, were converted by Borco-Höhns in Rotenburg/Wümme (near Hanover) and feature a dividing sliding door between the cab and the rear section as well as a sales flap and counter. The liveried vehicles shown here were part of the sales fleet used by the coffee company Tchibo.

A TRIO OF DESSERTS

RIGHT: This original paint/signwriting 1964 SO 2 was formerly a Bavarian Mobile Shop for the bakery Albert Dürr. It is now a working Ice Cream Van owned by a collector.

BELOW: A beautifully restored Late Bay Ice Cream Van brings a smile to everyone's face.

BOTTOM: This T3 Ice Cream Van was pictured at the Hanover Anniversary event in 2007

FLORIDA BOY ORANGE

44

KO·BK 561H

10

SO and special body pick-up trucks

As well as being a versatile, reliable, multi-purpose vehicle in its own right, the Pick-Up has had more SO and special body conversions than any other model, as can be seen in the SO listing below.

- SO 8 Wide Bed Pick-Up, metal (until 1958)
- SO 9 Wide Bed Pick-Up, wood (until 1958)
- SO 8 Pick-Up (Cherry Picker) with hydraulic lifting platform V90 (largest size)
- SO 9 Pick-Up with smaller hydraulic lifting platform V80 (Cherry Picker)
- SO 10 Pick-Up with single person hydraulic lifting platform V60
- SO 11 Pick-Up Ladder Truck
- SO 12 Pick-Up Box Wagen with aluminium roll shutter doors

- SO 13 Pick-Up with enclosed storage box
- SO 14 Box Trailer and mounting for Pick-Up Bed for carrying long poles/pipes
- SO 15 Tipper Truck
- SO 24 pole-carrying trailer (no storage) and mounting
- SO 25 Pick-Up Low Loader
- SO 31 Heating Oil Delivery Pick-Up with tank and dispenser pump
- SO 32 Enclosed Box Van similar to SO 12 but with roll shutter access

Work on designing a flat bed, load-carrying (Pick-Up Truck) version of the new VW Transporter had started in 1949, when the second generation of prototypes was being designed, and with the introduction of the Single Cab Pick-Up in August 1952 the range

of commercial applications greatly increased. Two main body modifications were made to the original production buses – the spare wheel was moved from the engine bay to behind the passenger seat and the fuel tank was moved from the right side of the engine compartment to above the rear axle. This allowed the engine compartment area to be flattened so that the cargo bed could run the full length of the vehicle. A storage area under the load bed was also created and accessed by a side lid; this was extremely useful for keeping tools and equipment secure and was called a 'treasure chest' in promotional material.

Such was the versatility and popularity of this Pick-Up that in just five months of production in 1952 it took seven per cent of the total Transporter

production for the full year. In fact, right through to 1967 approximately twenty per cent of all Transporter production every year was a form of Pick-Up. Interestingly, the first bus to roll off the new Hanover assembly line on 9 March 1956 was a Dove Blue Pick-Up. Realizing the popularity of the Binz Double Cab, Volkswagen launched its own factory Double Cab model (Doka) in September 1958.

From the start of production the Pick-Up's flat load area provided an ideal platform for adapting it to specialist uses such as mounting ladder rigs, while treasure chest lockers were ideal for fitting any hydraulic equipment, for example on Tipper Truck conversions. The Pick-Up also offered the ideal base for coachbuilt, special purpose bodies including enclosed areas for Box Container Vans or Hearses, equipment for carrying sheet glass or bottles, or conversion for use as snow ploughs, refuse collection and street cleaners.

The popularity of the VW Pick-Up Truck, and the seemingly infinite number of uses it can be adapted to, has continued through succeeding generations. With the introduction of the T4, Volkswagen also offered a cab and chassis-only version specifically for special body additions, as well as Single and Double Cab models.

These 1952 images, showing two very different uses for the Pick-Up as glass carrier and drinks delivery van, appeared in the 1955 Special Interiors brochure.

The popularity of the Pick-Up model for varied commercial uses has carried through to the T5, and Volkswagen continues to use licensed and approved convertors for its latest generation of Special Bodies. Under the heading 'Engineered to Go', Volkswagen UK publicity and sales brochures introduce them as 'the ideal platform for a wide variety of specialist applications – from tippers to boxes, dropsides to refrigerated bodies, the T5 forms the perfect foundation.' Pick-Up versions of the Crafter, successor to the LT, is now a popular choice for tippers, Lutons and dropside (Pick-Up) conversions and, with the introduction of Volkswagen's Amarok Pick-Up SUV in 2011 aimed at the commercial and leisure markets, the range is complete. The looks may have changed but not the versatility for the job.

The drinks delivery van features an enclosed, shelved load area with roll-down tarpaulin sides.

The "Moortown" Multi-Purpose Conversions to the Volkswagen Transporter

MOORTOWN MOTORS LIMITED
Yorkshire Distributors for Volkswagen

THE MOORTOWN MULTI-PURPOSE CONVERSION

Moortown Motors was a Yorkshire (UK) based company, best known for its bespoke cabinet built camping conversions. These 1958 brochures show that the company also produced a range of commercial Special Bodies based on the Pick-Up. The Mark 1, with open sides, was for milk delivery. The Mark 2 had a fully enclosed compartment, similar to the SO 12 Koffer-Aufbau, but with three steel sliding doors on each side. The Mark 3 was basically the same as the Mark 2, but with a full width opening rear tailgate, allowing access on three sides. Various forms of interior shelving and racks to suit businesses such as bakeries and confectioners were available as options.

The MARK I for MILK DELIVERY. Recommended load—740 pints in standard crates. Underfloor compartment ideal for poultry and eggs.

The MARK II for BREAD DELIVERY. Suggested loading—36 standard trays (30″ x 18″)—8″ between centres.

The MARK I for GREENGROCERY. Excellent display value. Underfloor compartment for bulk storage.

Examples of Volkswagen Versatility

BELOW: Among the many Pick-Up variants shown in the 1962 brochure are a mobile milking parlour, wood wide bed with slatted side extensions, and heating oil delivery truck.

This 1961 Florida Boy drinks delivery truck was supplied without side gates so crates had to be secured with straps.

BELOW: This specially equipped Double Cab was available to Volkswagen dealerships fully signwritten and kitted out to attend emergency breakdowns. Available as factory option M225 from 1962, equipment included winch, jacks, ripsaw, welding gear, and waterproof jacket and gumboots!

ABOVE: This Swedish Pick-Up features a lengthened load bed similar to the Kemperink.

ABOVE: This 1962 dealer information shows a telescopic lifting platform called 'The Giraffe'.

RIGHT: The Dutch firm Kemperink also produced extended length versions of both Single and Double Cab Pick-Up trucks.

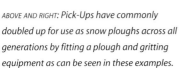

ABOVE AND RIGHT: Pick-Ups have commonly doubled up for use as snow ploughs across all generations by fitting a plough and gritting equipment as can be seen in these examples.

BELOW LEFT: This 1986 Syncro was equipped and used as a street cleaner.

BELOW RIGHT: A wide load platform can be used for many purposes, as in this T3 with mobile billboards.

The T4 Pick-Up was also available as a chassis base, allowing for many different Special Bodies to be mounted.

BELOW: This 1991 T4 Tipper conversion by Pfau could tip in three directions.

A specially lowered bed T4 Single Cab with load gantry and lockable tool box was designed to carry ladders. This conversion was produced by XM Systeme.

RIGHT: The standard T4 Pick-Up (dropside) featured a load gantry behind the cab to support uniformly distributed loads. This version features a factory option underbed 'treasure chest' locker.

The Pick-Up is ideally suited to market gardens and nurseries. This T4 version features a lower load bed.

A Double Cab T4 conversion kitted out especially for a locksmith and plumbing/heating engineer is based on the old SO 12 Box Van, and features top hinged side and rear access.

ABOVE: UK convertors Ingimex Ltd offer a Crafter dropside flat bed load carrier with load gantry behind the cab.

RIGHT: The Crafter body is now used for UK Pick-Up style body conversions such as Tipper Trucks, also converted by Ingimex Ltd.

Factory publicity shot emphasizing the rugged nature of the Crafter Pick-Up.

BELOW: The popularity of the Tipper Truck conversion has continued onto the T5 platform.

Factory promotional shot of the T5 Double Cab Pick-Up in action. Note the underbed optional 'treasure chest'.

BELOW: The new Amarok Double Cab Pick-Up is designed to suit both commercial and leisure uses.

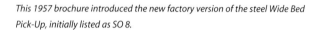
VW-Pritschenwagen mit verbreiterter Ladefläche (SO 8)

This 1957 brochure introduced the new factory version of the steel Wide Bed Pick-Up, initially listed as SO 8.

This August 1965 Westfalia version shows the wood bed/sides M201 option, complete with full tarp and bows. Note the special longer mirror arms. The Pick-Up is still owned by its original owner.

SO 8/SO 9 WIDE BED PICK-UP (M200/M201)

A metal version of the Wide Bed Pick-Up was available from 1956 made by Fritz Herrmann of Marburg. This became SO 8 with the new designations introduced in 1957, and another version, made by Westfalia, with wood sidegates and floor, was also listed, designated SO 9.

However, for 1958 Volkswagen introduced the Pick-Up with extended load area, or wide bed, as a factory model with its own M code, and the previous SO designation was discontinued

in Volkswagen listings. It came in two options – a factory all-steel bed and side gates (M200) or a wooden bed/gates version made by Westfalia (M201). The factory metal version was wider than the wood Westfalia version, but the wood version offered slightly longer load space (the rear overhangs) and the side gates were two centimetres higher. The steel bed version was lined with wood slats, while the wood version had a flat wooden floor.

Both wider bed models offered more carrying capacity for bulkier or awkward loads, and proved especially popular with both the construction and agricultural businesses. As well as

alterations to the load bed and new front panels where the bed joins the cab, the conversion also necessitated a new size rear tailgate and longer arms to mount the side mirrors on. Optional equipment included re-sized tarp and bows set up and twin bed lockers.

BAY WINDOW WIDE BEDS

The steel wide bed option was discontinued with the introduction of the new Bay Window models in August 1967, but the extended wood platform/sides, produced by Westfalia, continued as M201.

Built in 1969 and converted by Westfalia, this was one of the first Bay Window versions and was formerly part of the now defunct Westfalia Museum. Note the different style of extended mirror arms.

This Late Bay version features a rare, specially sized, tarp and bows option.

1980 T3 WIDE BED

Westfalia continued to offer a Wide Bed conversion for the T3 range. The version shown here was built in 1980 and came with Hella fog lamps, special wide bed mirrors, towing hitch, twin bed lockers with lights inside each and a fold-down step on the rear gate. It also features bespoke wooden slide-out drawers in the treasure chest compartments, which though not original Westfalia equipment, are a very useful modification. Finished in Orient Red with black bumpers and wheel rims, it was built for the German market with the 1.6-litre petrol engine fitted with a governor – a set up suited to local deliveries only! It came up for sale on eBay in 2005 and now resides in the USA, where it is owned by enthusiast Randy Coburn.

ABOVE: Hella fog lamps were fitted from new on this 1980 Westfalia Wide Bed.

BELOW LEFT: A Westfalia tow hitch and twin underbed lockers were also factory-fitted options.

BELOW RIGHT: Finished in Orient Red with black bumpers and wheel rims, it was built for the German market with the 1.6-litre petrol engine fitted with a governor.

LEFT: The lockers have been fitted with bespoke wooden slide-out drawers, which, though not original Westfalia equipment, are a very useful modification.

BELOW LEFT: Special extension mirror arms are necessary for rear vision.

BELOW: The Westfalia-built Wide Beds had wood side gates and floor.

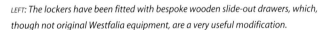

1967 STEEL WIDE BED M200

The Velvet Green M200 example shown here was built on 31 June 1967, on chassis number 267 132 613, and shipped to Italy on 4 July. Its history over the years is unclear but it was eventually unearthed in a barn and brought to England by a bus enthusiast in 1992. Although the truck was running, it was rough, the paint was very faded, the wooden bed runners were rotting and there were patches of rust. In 1994 it was sold on, but the new owner died just after starting a restoration of the chassis and bodywork and it went into storage. In 2003 the owner's ex-girlfriend, who had been heavily involved with the restoration project, took on the task of finishing the Pick-Up.

ABOVE LEFT: *This steel Wide Bed Pick-Up (M200) was built in June 1967, near the end of T1 production.*

ABOVE: *Wider bed models offered more carrying capacity for bulkier or awkward loads, and proved especially popular with construction and agricultural businesses.*

BELOW: *The factory metal version was wider than the wood Westfalia version.*

ABOVE: *Because of the increased width, specially extended mirror arms were fitted.*

The front panel 'bib', for protection from stone chips, is a modern addition, not a period accessory.

The steel bed version was lined with wood slats, while the wood version had a flat wooden floor.

RIGHT: From the rear the extra width created by the overhanging sides can be seen clearly.

BELOW: The bus was built for the Italian market, hence the Italian spec side flashers.

BELOW: The Pick-Up has been painstakingly restored with close attention to correct period detail; for example, the wood slats were machined with the same profile as the originals and riveted in place.

VW-Pritschenwagen
mit hydraulischer Hebebühne

SO 8/9/10: PICK-UP WITH HYDRAULIC LIFTING PLATFORM

As SO 8 and SO 9 (Wide Bed Pick-Up) had become M-coded factory models in 1958, these spare SO designations were now given to the hydraulic lifting platform set up commonly known as Cherry Pickers. Introduced in 1960, these were based on a Single Cab Pick-Up and featured a hydraulically operated lifting platform that could be rotated through 360 degrees as well as reaching an almost vertical position. This flexible reach meant it was especially popular with market gardeners, municipal authorities and power companies. Several sizes of lifting platform were available, each identified by an SO and V number:

- SO 8: lifting platform V90 (largest size)
- SO 9: lifting platform V80
- SO 10: lifting platform V60 (single person version).

The firm Ruthmann-Steiger, which specialized in hydraulic engineering

RIGHT: Factory promotional shot of the 1960 demonstration model showing how effective the vehicle is for overhead cable repairs. Note the original WOB 717 plate.

and equipment, was responsible for the actual body conversion that was ordered from Volkswagen dealerships via the special body (SO) models catalogue. A standard Pick-Up, supplied without side gates (M118) was fitted with hydraulically operated stabilizing/levelling legs in a steel frame. The legs operate independently, allowing the load bed to sit perfectly level, and the rotating/lifting crane arm, with a small enclosed platform, is mounted onto the load bed just behind the cab. A fixed ladder section at the open rear of the enclosed platform gives

BELOW: Another factory shot of the same demonstration vehicle, fitted with a larger platform and new licence plate WOB 04001.

easy access and the operator controls height and angle directly via the control panel mounted in the front. Apart from electrics, switches and hydraulic cables, no major body modifications were needed, and the whole set up could be removed from the load bed fairly easily. Because the stabilizing platform/legs protruded beyond the sides of the vehicle body, two warning poles, mounted on springs, were fitted to the front bumper, giving the driver a clear sense of the overall width.

ABOVE: This restored 1960 Cherry Picker was the original factory demonstration model.

ABOVE: SO 10 was the V60 (single person lifting platform) model.

1960 SO 10

The model featured here is particularly interesting as it was the prototype model, commissioned by Volkswagen in 1960 and based at Wolfsburg for much of its life, where it was used as a demonstration vehicle and for publicity and brochure shots. Built in September 1960 and originally finished in Light Grey, like all models used as demonstrators or prototypes by the factory, it carried the distinctive WOB licence plate, showing its Wolfsburg registration and origin. During its time as a promotional vehicle, Volkswagen experimented with several different sizes of platform and had registration numbers other than the original WOB V 717 plate, as can be seen in the factory archive promotional photographs overleaf. What happened to the vehicle after Volkswagen sold it on is unclear, but it did see use by a market gardener before passing into the hands of a bus enthusiast in 1991. He kept it for some years and carried out some restoration before it was acquired in 2006 by Markus Adam, who owns Adam GmbH, a company specializing in hiring out and supplying hydraulic lifting platforms, equipment and specialist vehicles.

His workshop team carried out a ground up restoration, using original parts wherever possible, before repainting it in Fire Truck Red (RAL 300) and White, which are the company colours. Ruthmann's (which is still in business) were even able to supply some correct original parts as well as give advice on suitable alternatives. Now just one of three surviving examples known to be in safe working condition, and the only one in such perfect condition, life for this commercial Bulli has come full circle. It started its life as a promotional vehicle for Volkswagen and now it is continuing that tradition promoting a modern-day business and attracting admiring looks wherever it is seen.

BELOW: Operation of the mechanism is from the enclosed platform, as Markus proudly demonstrates.

ABOVE: Before the platform is raised, hydraulic feet operate independently to provide stability and ensure the load bed is level. As can be seen here, this may mean lifting a wheel off the ground.

ABOVE: Because the whole set up is mounted on the load bed no major body modifications were needed, and it could be removed easily.

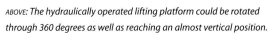
ABOVE: The hydraulically operated lifting platform could be rotated through 360 degrees as well as reaching an almost vertical position.

ABOVE: Now just one of three surviving examples known to be in safe working condition, it is the only one in such perfect condition.

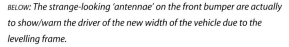
BELOW: The strange-looking 'antennae' on the front bumper are actually to show/warn the driver of the new width of the vehicle due to the levelling frame.

BELOW: The lifting platform is accessed at the rear via a small ladder and operated from a control panel inside the platform.

Vom richtigen Arbeitsgerät hängt vieles ab. Gute und schnelle Arbeit, angemessener Verdienst, prompter Kundendienst – kurz: die Leistungsfähigkeit des ganzen Betriebes steht und fällt mit ihm.
Wie ist es damit bei Unternehmen, die vorwiegend in luftiger Höhe zu arbeiten haben? Mit der Leiter allein ist es nicht getan – sie muß erst einmal an Ort und Stelle sein! Naheliegende Lösung: mit einem fahrbaren Untersatz verbinden!
Erfolg: Rationeller Arbeitseinsatz und Wendigkeit in der Planung. Die Termine können eingehalten, neue Auftraggeber dazugewonnen werden. Der Betrieb bekommt größere „Reichweite", unvorhergesehene Situationen lassen sich leichter meistern.

VW-Pritschenwagen mit Drehleiter-Aufbau

VW – millionenfach erfahren in der Lösung vielfältigster Transportprobleme – hat auch hierfür das richtige Fahrzeug entwickelt:
VW-Pritschenwagen mit Drehleiteraufbau.
Er erfüllt die Wünsche der Elektrizitätswerke, Überlandzentralen, der kommunalen Betriebe, der Straßenbahngesellschaften, der Neon-Spezialfirmen und Gebäude-Reinigungsunternehmen nach einem zweckmäßigen, beweglichen und damit wirtschaftlichen Arbeitsgerät.

ABOVE: Volkswagen's SO brochures often had a distinctive dove blue stripe styling feature, as in this 1962 Ladder Truck brochure.

SO 11: PICK-UP WITH TURNTABLE LADDER

The Ladder Truck, designated SO 11, was produced by the firm Meyer-Hagen, which had been founded in the town of Hagen in 1886. The firm mainly produced fire-fighting equipment, ladders and pumps and also fitted out Fire Trucks to order, complete with hoses and mobile pumps. From the early 1950s they also began to supply and fit turntable ladders that could be fitted to the bed of a VW Pick-Up truck, a conversion which soon found favour with municipal authorities, roofers, tree surgeons, overhead cable repair firms and power companies as well as local and factory fire services. The ten-metre extendable ladder was made from wood with steel reinforcements and was fitted to a hand-operated turntable, allowing it to swivel through 360 degrees. For stability and support a metal frame was fixed at the rear in place of the rear bumper and featured foldout legs that were wound down by hand. When in transit the ladder folded down and hung over the cab.

Other companies also produced turntable Ladder Trucks, such as Magirus Deutz, which offered a steel ladder option. Similar conversions were also offered by several European companies, including the Ben Pon dealership.

Dating from 1958, this Magirus Deutz Ladder Truck conversion features all-steel ladders.

A 1961 Meyer-Hagen ready for restoration.

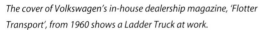

The cover of Volkswagen's in-house dealership magazine, 'Flotter Transport', from 1960 shows a Ladder Truck at work.

Period photograph showing semaphored 1959 Ladder Truck at work.

1956 LADDER TRUCK

This Meyer-Hagen Ladder Truck was built in August 1956 on chassis number 194 943, though the designation SO 11 would not be used until 1957. Finished in Dove Blue, and carrying optional orange flashing roof light and pole-mounted spotlight on the cab rear, it was ordered by Pfalzwerke AG (a Rhineland power company), which used it for overhead electric cable maintenance until February 1966. It was then used by two other owners before being laid up in April 1970. At some point later it was owned by a museum. Ulrich Seibel acquired it in October 1992 in a poor but roadworthy condition. He spent two years fully restoring it to its original condition before it debuted at Bad Camberg in 1995; it now attends exhibitions and special events.

ABOVE: Immaculately restored, this 1956 version is one of the earliest known examples.

LEFT: The bumper-mounted small flashing indicators (front and rear) have been added for safety reasons but are removable for exhibition.

BELOW: The flashing orange roof light and pole-mounted spotlight are original equipment.

1963 SO 11

The Ladder Truck featured here was built as a Single Cab Pick-Up on 20 October 1963, with factory-fitted options of no side gates (M118), steering/ignition lock (M056), axle weight plates (M065) and the new 1500cc engine/1 tonne payload option (M215). It was then delivered to the Hanover Volkswagen dealer Bischoff & Hamel, who installed the turntable ladder supplied by Meyer-Hagen. They also fitted a flashing blue light, twin Klaxon horns and a pole-mounted emergency spotlight. Unusually, the Pick-Up was finished in Ruby Red (L456) as opposed to Fire Truck Red, suggesting it was probably ordered by a factory or plant for its private use as first line defence. The bumpers were also painted with warning/high visibility red/white stripes.

Little is known about its working life, but it ended up in a Film Museum as a set prop before being found by Bulli enthusiast and Bulli Kartei member, Guido Boes. He carried out a two-year ground up restoration of body and ladder mechanisms, before fully repainting inside and out in the original Ruby Red, with the load bed finished in silver.

ABOVE: Twin Bosch horns are mounted on the front bumper and a pole-mounted emergency spotlight on the cab front end.

BELOW: Stability is provided by winding down the steel frame fitted at the rear where the bumper would normally sit.

LEFT: Ropes, pulleys and cogs – simple but very effective technology operated by hand.

1965 FRENCH CONVERSION

This 1965 Pick-Up was exported to France and converted as a Ladder Truck by the Echelles Vadot company in Lyon. The 'Voiture Nachelle', as it is called in France, started life for an electric engineering company, Francois Meloux, who had a contract to maintain overhead power lines near the city of Montpellier. Later, in the mid 1980s, the truck was used by the company to install Christmas lighting in the local town.

In the mid 1990s it was bought by a company employee, who reluctantly passed it on to Bob van Heyst of BBT in Belgium in 1999; it arrived at his home on his birthday! He has since carried out a full restoration to remove dents and repainted it in the original Light Grey with the original signwriting. The original wood on the ladder has been carefully dismantled and re-varnished, and the fully working bus is now a regular visitor and attraction at major shows and events in Europe.

ABOVE LEFT: *Split Bus Nation 2010*

ABOVE RIGHT: *Bad Camberg 2007*

LEFT: *Bad Camberg 1999*

RIGHT: *Hessisch Oldendorf 2009*

1970 T2 CONVERSION

T3 LADDER TRUCKS

ABOVE: *This hydraulically operated Ladder Truck was a factory demonstration model based on a 1986 Syncro.*

RIGHT: *This battered T3 Meyer-Hagen Ladder Truck was spotted still working at the side of the road ten years ago, but is now sadly no more.*

LEFT: *This 1970 Ladder Truck's origins are obscure, but it uses an SO 8 Wide Bed Pick-Up as the base. The rear stability frame is non-standard, suggesting an unofficial conversion.*

SO and special body pick-up trucks

The introduction of the Pick-Up in 1952 led to another version of the original Lieferwagen (Delivery/Panel Van). Known as Koffer-Aufbau (literally luggage box), these vans consisted of a coachbuilt enclosed box container sited on the Pick-Up load bed. The *Special Interiors* brochure of 1955 showed two versions; one with steel doors and one with twin aluminium roll shutters on each side. Both date from 1953 and were box shaped with flat roofs.

Versions of Box Delivery Vans continued through to the late 1980s when the need for larger load capacity meant the small Koffer-Aufbau gradually gave way to Luton Top versions, the LT, and in 2007 the new generation of Crafter.

The first SO listing in 1957 had three variants of Koffer-Aufbau:

- SO 12 Pick-Up Box Wagon with aluminium roll shutter doors (Felix Striepke)
- SO 13 Pick-Up with enclosed storage box (Westfalia)
- SO 32 Enclosed Box Van similar to SO 12 but with twin roll shutter access (Felix Striepke).

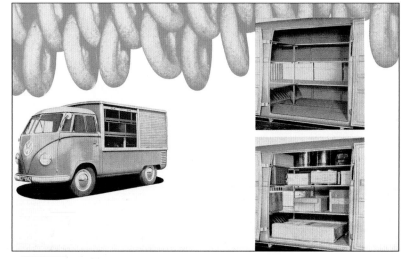

TOP TO BOTTOM:

1957 brochure showing the single roll shutter door version SO 12.

SO 13 was an Enclosed Box Van, made by Westfalia, as seen in this 1961 brochure.

A 1955 brochure showed this 1953/54 Pick-Up version with two aluminium roll shutter doors, which would become SO 32 in 1957 (SO 12 had a single roll shutter each side).

Another pre-1954 Pick-Up featuring an enclosed box with steel twin opening side and rear doors, later designated SO 13.

The Westfalia version, SO 13, was all metal and featured full-height twin rear doors and a single door at the side front end. The box container was less angular, with a shaped roof giving slightly increased headroom. Another version featuring different configurations of single or twin roll-up aluminium shutter doors, SO 32 and SO 12, was available from Felix Striepke, and was especially popular with the fire service.

By 1963 SO 12 was no longer listed separately, and from 1964 both SO 13 and SO 32 were no longer listed as SO models; instead they were now grouped under the section showing further ideas and possible special body variants (Anregungen, *see* page 17). From 1967 the roll shutter door version was designated SO 12.

This 1959 works photo of the factory demonstration SO 13 model clearly shows the wooden reinforcing slats in the interior.

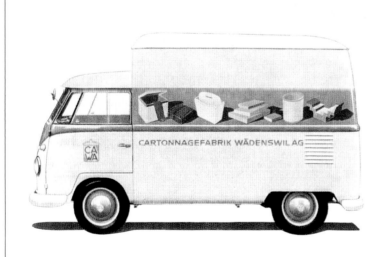

ABOVE AND LEFT: *These examples of liveried and signwritten Koffer-Aufbau appeared in a brochure devoted to showcase the potential for advertising offered by the smooth Volkswagen surfaces. Vehicles from the UK and Switzerland are included here.*

RIGHT: *Based on SO 13, this Italian version was built to order in 1962 for use by a market trader specializing in fabrics and material. The side opening and rear flaps are in two sections, with the top part hinging up to reveal shelving holding rolls of fabric, and the smaller lower section coming down to act as a sales counter. It also featured locker beds on both sides (M071), which stored extra rolls of fabric.*

The Pick-Up section in a 1962 brochure about special conversions included these examples of Koffer-Aufbau showing top hinged flap-up doors and roll shutter variants.

ABOVE: This High Roof factory prototype Karmann-built Koffer conversion dates from 1986 and was designated the Trader. One production option featured long vertical display windows.

CENTRE AND RIGHT: Many countries produced their own versions of SO models, based on the German versions, as in this 1962/63 example of an Italian version featuring top hinged flap doors.

SO and special body pick-up trucks

Listed in the first SO information in 1957 was a special trailer with long tow hitch arm, designed specifically to carry awkward, long loads such as poles and pipes. It was available in two versions: SO 14 was a heavy-duty wheeled trailer or Nachläufer (literally after-runner), produced by Gebrüder Wolperding and later by Westfalia, while SO 24 ('Stückgut- und Langmaterial-Anhänger', literally parcels and long materials trailer), manufactured by Josef Fickers, was a box trailer based version giving additional carrying space for equipment. Wheels for each version were the standard 15-inch (14-inch from December 1963) Volkswagen versions with Volkswagen logo hubcaps. Both versions came with a mounting for the poles that fitted onto the load bed. Although mainly marketed and sold to accompany Pick-Up trucks, both Double and Single Cabs, the mounting could also be fitted on the bed above the engine so that the trailer could be used with a Panel Van, Kombi or Microbus (although the rear tailgate had to remain open). Because the mounting was easily removable, the base vehicle could be used for carrying other loads.

The Pole Carrier was especially popular with builders, construction companies and municipal authorities and, as can be seen below, the versatility of the Pick-Up base for moving very long loads has continued through the different model generations.

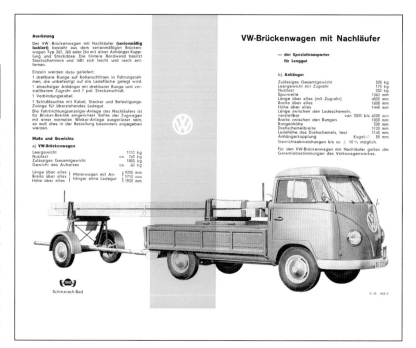

1959 brochure showing SO 14; a heavy-duty wheeled trailer, or Nachläufer (literally after-runner).

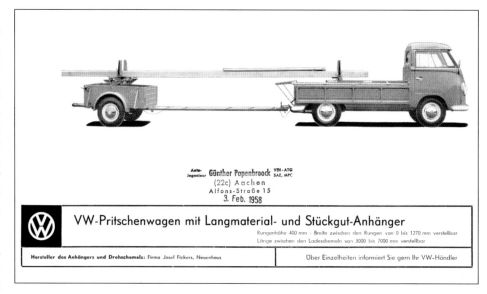

1957 brochure showing SO 24, a box trailer and mounting called the 'Stückgut- und Langmaterial-Anhänger' (literally parcels and long materials trailer).

BELOW: Factory shot showing SO 14 with the load bed mounting frame clearly visible.

ABOVE LEFT: Period photograph from around 1960 showing a Double Cab and Pole Carrier at work.

ABOVE RIGHT: Newly restored 1963 Double Cab and Westfalia-built SO 14 trailer on show at the 60th Anniversary International Volkswagen Bus Convention in Hanover, 2007. (Note: The Doka has been lowered and safari windows added.)

ABOVE: A fully restored combination of a 1977 Double Cab, used by Hanover Town Council, with a 1969 SO 14 Pole Carrier on show at the 60th Anniversary International Volkswagen Bus Convention in Hanover, 2007.

ABOVE: The trailer was built by Gebrüder Wolperding.

LEFT: For the T3 generation a heavy-duty version of SO 14, with twin axles to cope with heavy loads, was available. This period photograph shows a 1986 Single Cab at work in a logging yard.

RIGHT: This 1986 Pick-Up has a large open box trailer version of SO 24, which maximizes versatility with easily removable carrying frame, enabling the trailer to be used for other purposes.

SO 15 HYDRAULIC TIPPER TRUCK

Autodienst Promotor GmbH, based in Lengerich, converted Pick-Up Trucks to Tipper Trucks for both the T1 and T2 models. They were designated as SO 15 and delivered from the factory with side gates not fitted (M64) and with supplied wood slats not fixed to the load bed (M57). Using the factory-supplied side and rear gates and an additional load bed floor, a complete new body section was fabricated and fitted to the Pick-Up body with tippable bearings at the rear. Raising and lowering the bed was by hand-pump operation of a hydraulic ram, which could raise the new bed by forty-five degrees. The hydraulic mechanisms and pump were located in the locker bed. Because of the extra weight of the new load bed and hydraulic mechanisms the maximum payload was reduced to 860 kilograms. Promotor's T1 (Split) versions were available from 1960 and T2 (Bay) versions were built from 1971 to 1979.

Bay Window Tipper Trucks were also converted by the Dutch dealership, Pons Automobielhandel from 1976, and in 1977 VW UK offered a version from PCS, 'The Tipmaster Electro Hydraulic Tipper'. Tipper Truck conversions were available for both T3 and T4 generations and have continued for the T5 Pick-Up and Crafter models.

1961 brochure showing the new Tipper special model.

ABOVE AND BELOW RIGHT: This 1967 Tipper Truck was converted by a firm in Verona, Italy, and features a hydraulic system powered by the engine, instead of a hand pump.

BELOW: Archive photograph showing a T1 Tipper at work on a refuse dump.

Works photograph of the new T2 Tipper conversion dating from 1973.

This 1977 factory demonstration model of a UK conversion was made by Tipmaster for VW UK. Known as the Dustmaster, it was specifically designed for refuse collection. Tipmaster is still a Volkswagen-approved converter, now offering T5 Tipper conversions

LEFT AND BELOW: This 1986 T3 Double Cab Tipper Truck used a Syncro base and was a factory demonstration model.

LEFT: By the time of the T4 the hydraulic systems on Tipper conversions were powered electrically, not manually

LEFT: Council workers using the capabilities of a Doka Tipper Truck in 1985. Manual operation is still in use on this model.

LEFT: Note how the tipping load bed overhangs at the rear because of the Double Cab.

BELOW: A Doka version of the tarp and bows was supplied as optional equipment.

1978 DOUBLE CAB TIPPER

Normally a Single Cab was used for T2 Tippers, but in October 1978 a small number of Double Cab versions were built for the Hanover municipal authority by Promotor. The Tipper shown here is the only one of these Double Cab versions known to survive. Finished in Brilliant Orange, it features a steel-framed wooden load bed, which overhangs at the rear and is complete with tarp and bows. The City authorities sold it on in 1994 and it was then used to transport excavator buckets to and from building sites until 2001. It was due to be traded in (and scrapped by the dealer) but was rescued at the last minute by bus enthusiast Thomas Ebke.

LEFT: Normally Single Cabs were used on T2 Tippers; this is one of a few specially built for the Hanover City Council.

LEFT: The load bed and sides were wood with a metal frame.

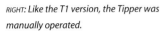

RIGHT: Like the T1 version, the Tipper was manually operated.

LEFT: Andreas Plogmaker demonstrates the versatility of the conversion.

RIGHT: Finished in Municipal Orange, it saw service in Hanover until 1994. It was then used on a building site, and finally rescued from being scrapped in 2001.

ABOVE: *This T3 Tipper was converted by Karmann in 1983.*

LEFT: *The hydraulics on this version are powered electrically instead of manually.*

BELOW: *A hydraulic ram raises and lowers the bed. All the mechanisms are sited under the load bed.*

1983 T3 KARMANN TIPPER

This conversion was carried out by Karmann in the VW-Werk in Osnabrück and based on a standard Model 245 Single Cab Pick-Up. Though similar in design and construction to the earlier versions, this differs in that the hydraulics are powered by the battery via a switch sited in the cab behind the driver. The current used to operate the tipper is such that, even if the battery will not start the engine, it will still operate the tipper hydraulics.

The tipper featured here was ordered new in 1983 by a small family market garden business based in Lenz, Germany. The customer specifically requested the option of twin locker doors for the underbed storage to allow access from either side, and also opening quarter lights, dash clock, six-digit speedometer with trip meter and a radio. Finished in Timor Beige, it was powered by the new 1.9-litre water-cooled petrol engine; considering the vehicle was a workhorse it was surprising the diesel engine option was not taken up! In 2005 Roland Knauss, Michael Molk and Günther Mack heard this very rare Volkswagen was up for sale by the son, who now ran the family business, and promptly acquired it and put it to work for Günther's house renovation. It was then re-sprayed in its original colour, after some minor rust repairs, and the mechanics were overhauled so that another piece of special model history could be preserved.

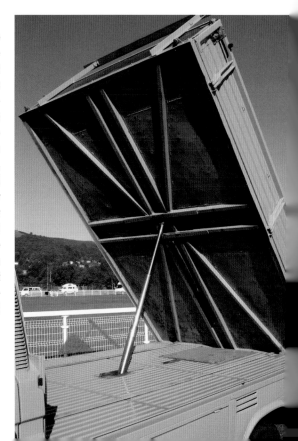

RIGHT: Despite a hard working life for a market garden, the vehicle is in excellent working order.

CENTRE: The twin locker door factory option was specified by the original buyer to enable access from either side.

BELOW: When not a Tipper, the vehicle returns to a load-carrying Pick-Up.

VW-Tieflader

SO 25 LOW LOADER PICK-UP (TIEFLADER)

Despite its load-carrying capacity the Pick-Up's high bed did not readily lend itself to large and bulky objects being easily loaded by hand. Some businesses needed an easy way to roll on/roll off awkward loads.

SO 25

In 1960 Westfalia introduced their special body version based on the Pick-Up Truck – the Tieflader (Low Loader). Designated SO 25, no working pre-1967 versions are known to survive, although some are awaiting major restoration! It was designed specifically for carrying awkward loads and the body had special modifications with two opening side 'doors'. The side panels and gates were cut and welded to fabricate 'doors', which were then hinged behind the cab. The original load bed was also cut and the front section hinged to flap back onto the rear of the load bed. This allowed the Pick-Up bed to be used either in its original position or to create a lower section, using the space where the lockers were normally sited to carry tools and large boxes or containers. Extra flexibility was created by the use of a foldout frame with runners and sled, up which bulky loads could be slid and placed onto this lower section of the bed. This frame had cushioned sections to protect the load. A full tarp and bows set up and removable metal storage boxes were optional extras.

The Tieflader offered the ability to transport large items such as commercial fridges quickly and easily, without the need for hydraulic lifting platforms, and was also especially popular with municipal authorities for their road gangs. This version had an orange flashing light and metal bin in the low section for carrying gravel or sand, with a small tarp and bows over for protection.

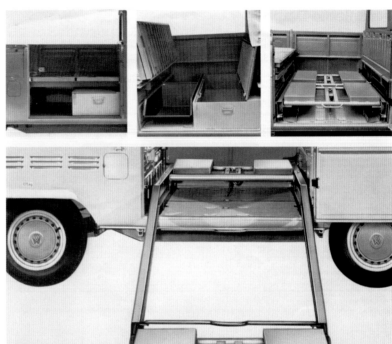

CENTRE: Close-up images from 1972 show the fold-up frame with cushion supports or used with slide-out trays and toolbox in the underbed locker space.

RIGHT: Publicity image from 1972 showing the Tieflader being used by a road gang.

THE T4 RAZORBACK

With advances in engineering and materials by the time of the T4, the Low Loader had evolved into a very different vehicle: the Razorback. (Razorback is the patent name for an innovative, special bodied, ground-loading commercial, developed by the parent company in Australia.) A prototype demonstrator Razorback conversion was built for VW AG in 2000, featuring a coachbuilt Box Delivery Van, built on the T4 cab and chassis option, with a hydraulically operated, complete inner cargo area and floor.

Also in 2000, VW Commercial UK commissioned an LWB Pick-Up Razorback conversion from the Razorback Company in Coventry as its own demonstrator and publicity vehicle.

The Razorback Pick-Up features a hydraulically operated floor that lowers to give direct roll-on access from the street. Inside the load bed is a complete inner box section, which can be lowered to the floor while the rear tailgate flaps down level to the ground, thus making rolling kegs or drums onto the bed very easy. To accommodate the lifting hydraulics and reinforced heavy-duty lifting bed section, the side panels have been widened and strengthened. The circular side doors allow access to the spare wheel and lifting gear. There is also a one-tonne winch and tow bar set up mounted on a frame behind the cab, so that pallets or containers can be winched into the load bed area ready for transport. Operation is simply by turning a switch on the rear side panel; when activated the floor tray section moves down while the tailgate simultaneously drops open. A warning buzzer sounds if one tries to close the doors before the floor is fully retracted back up into the driving position.

In 2000 VW AG in Hanover commissioned a demonstration model of a Delivery Van fitted with Razorback conversion.

The Razorback, developed in Australia, featured a hydraulically operated inner floor, which dropped to ground level for easy loading.

Although it was built specifically for Volkswagen in 2000 for use as an exhibition vehicle, when the T5 came along just three years later, its fuel tank was sited in a different place to the T4, meaning the Razorback lifting mechanisms would no longer fit. So Volkswagen put it up for sale and it was promptly bought by Martin Brook, still with only 8,000 miles on the clock and in near perfect condition. He runs a biodiesel company, recycling vegetable oil as fuel, and the vehicle, with its roll-on/roll-off facility, is ideal for collecting waste oil in large drums.

A Razorback Pick-Up exhibition vehicle was built for VW UK, also in 2000.

To accommodate the lifting hydraulics and reinforced heavy-duty lifting bed section, the side panels have been widened and strengthened.

Inside the load bed is a complete inner box section, which can be lowered to the floor.

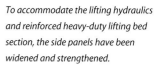

As the floor lowers, the tailgate simultaneously flaps down level to the ground.

1961 USA LOW LOADER CONVERSION

Around 1961 a conversion firm in America came up with its own version of a Low Loader, clearly inspired by SO 25, but with a lower front floor section accessed by a ramp made by folding down a side door. Very little is known about the conversion, though reliable sources suggest that only fifty were built, with just three known to survive.

Single Cabs with twin lockers (treasure chests) were used, so a complete lower floor space was available. The load bed area above this was then removed and the under chassis strengthened. The left locker door was welded shut and the right side gate was cut and welded to the right locker door to make a new door, with additional bracing at the join, and hinged at the bottom to act as a ramp. The inside of this was then faced with metal to allow smooth access. A wooden frame divided the raised and lower sections, with additional wood slat protection on the bulkhead.

The restored model shown here was built on 13 December 1960 and finished in Light Grey with American market preparations (such as sealed beam headlights), before being exported to the USA via Los Angeles and then converted. Its current owner, Don McNeal, has fully restored it and had it repainted in yellow as a classic Coca Cola delivery vehicle, complete with 'faded' signwriting and logos for a period effect as well as an original style Coca Cola roundel and logo on the front panel. The Coca Cola Company made extensive use of VW models in the 1960s, including SO 25 Low Loaders, and the livery recreates the look of one of these perfectly.

This US-built version of SO 25, originally in Light Grey, was converted in 1961.

It has been repainted in yellow with 'faded' signwriting and logos, and an original style Coca Cola roundel to recreate the look of one of the original Coca Cola fleet.

ABOVE: The nearside locker door is welded up and the load bed area above the lockers removed to make a lowered floor section.

LEFT: Access to the lowered area is from the new offside door, hinged at the bottom to make a loading ramp.

SO and special body pick-up trucks

LEFT: A wooden frame divides the raised and lower sections, with additional wood slat protection on the bulkhead.

RIGHT: The shortened load bed still provides ample carrying space.

BELOW: The hubcaps have also been painted in authentic 1960s Coca Cola style.

RIGHT: The opening side door was made by cutting the right side gate and welding it to the right locker door, with additional bracing at the join.

SO and special body pick-up trucks

1969 WESTFALIA SO 25

The Bay Window SO 25 featured here rolled off the production line in August 1969 as a Single Cab Pick-Up and was delivered to the Westfalia-Werke for conversion as a Tieflader. The M plate has the M115 code, indicating factory preparations for the Low Loader conversion, and it was finished in Light Grey with black bumpers and wheels, with chrome hubcaps. It also features a mounting pole for a flashing warning light on the rear nearside of the cab. The fact that it was ordered and used by Volkswagen's Hanover factory (the M plate carries the VW factory destination code 910) suggests that it was one of the first of these new special bodied Pick-Ups on the T2 base, possibly even a prototype. Volkswagen used it for publicity pictures in their sales brochures and also as a demonstration vehicle at exhibitions. It was later used in the werks for carrying loads around the factory and site and in July 1971 it was equipped with a factory trailer coupling.

In 1983 it was acquired by the Malteser Hilfsdienst, an organization similar to the Red Cross, which attends disasters and accidents to bring relief and first aid. In 1989 an original tarp and bows was fitted to the complete rear bed section. The Malteser organization used it until 1990, when it passed to a private individual before ending up in a fire brigade museum, where it lay, forgotten, until in 2004 it was rescued and partially restored by Jörg Beckmann, a well-known Volkswagen enthusiast and parts dealer.

This is possibly the only surviving example from just two hundred Bay Window Tiefladers built, some of which were on the post 1973 updated T2b model.

Built in August 1969 and converted by Westfalia, this was a prototype/exhibition model used by the Hanover factory.

Twin opening side doors access a lowered floor area.

ABOVE: The original load bed above the lockers folds back to make the lower height section.

LEFT: The doors were hinged at the cab end allowing for open access on either or both sides.

Because the original load bed over the locker area is retained and hinged to fold back, the full original Pick-Up load bed space is available if required. Note the side door locks.

Twin locker versions were used and the side gates cut and welded to the locker doors to make new side doors. Note mounting pole for the flashing warning light on the cab rear.

ABOVE: This view shows the two different height load spaces with the load bed section folded back.

RIGHT: The folded-back section of the load bed can be seen clearly here.

LEFT: The swan neck Westfalia tow bar was added in 1971.

117

PICK-UP WITH HYDRAULIC LIFT CRANE

The version seen here (right) was the factory demonstration model, and shows the crane fitted to a wooden Wide Bed Single Cab.

1966 PROTOTYPE

Listed and described under Anregungen (suggestions) in 1966 dealership information, this Pick-Up featured a lifting crane mechanism fitted to the front right side behind the cab. Hydraulically powered, the standard fitting was a lifting hook attached to an elevating arm, in turn attached to a rotating mount that could turn through 360 degrees. Pullout stabilizing feet were fixed under the chassis section beneath the crane mechanism.

1970 AUSTRIAN CRANE LIFT

The Neptune Blue 1970 version below was built in Austria and features a removable, swivelling crane arm with manual lifting operation via a handle on the crane. The Pick-Up was supplied by the Austrian importer Porsche Konstruktionen KG and converted in November 1970 by Kartner Maschinenfabrik Egger, Villach. It was ordered by the firm Ignaz Piber, and was used mainly for transporting large agricultural machinery such as mowers. Fully restored and pictured here on display at the 60th Anniversary International Volkswagen Bus Convention in Hanover, it is now part of the Bulli Museum in Hessisch Oldendorf.

ABOVE: This 1987 Single Cab was a factory demonstration model (note WOB licence plate) and features a heavy-duty hydraulic crane lift made by HIAB.

T3 CRANE LIFTS

RIGHT: This T3 Syncro 4WD Doka with crane features a hydraulic mechanism similar to the 1960s versions and was spotted parked on the street in Germany.

T4 CONVERSIONS

BELOW: This factory photograph shows a T4, also with HIAB hydraulic lifting gear. Note the way the stabilizing foot swings out for added stability when in use.

JAGDWAGEN (HUNTER'S CAR)

RIGHT AND BELOW: 1988 Special Body 16-inch Syncro Double Cab

By the time of the T3, Volkswagen was producing fewer factory-built special conversions, instead relying on approved converters. The Jagdwagen, however, was created and equipped by Volkswagen itself.

In 1987 Volkswagen saw the potential market for a specialist hunting, leisure and forest management vehicle and, using a Syncro Double Cab as the base vehicle, created the Jagdwagen (Hunter's car). Initially it was advertised in the catalogue produced by Kettner (the market leader in hunting equipment) and the demonstration model shown was equipped with just about every extra conceivable. Such was its success that in 1988 Volkswagen produced their own Jagdwagen brochure extolling the luxurious leather interior, the fact that it was a smooth daily driver with rugged off-road capabilities, and had an extensive optional equipment list allowing a customer to tailor the vehicle to commercial or personal use.

The main selling point was the optional 16-inch wheel all-terrain package, available for all Syncros, giving greater ground clearance and more strength. Strengthening panels were welded into the chassis in strategic places to stiffen the body and plastic wheel arch flares fitted to cover up where VW/Steyr had to modify the rear edge of the wheel arches for clearance for the larger diameter wheels and tyres. Heavy-duty front and rear brakes, as used on the VW LT, were fitted, along with stronger shock absorbers and rear CV joints. A longer wheelbase was achieved by lengthening the rear trailing arms. The base package also included the external roll cage and front-mounted winch; everything else was chosen from the extensive optional equipment list, so each Jagdwagen was individually tailored to requirements. The cost of one vehicle that featured all the possible extras was around 100,000 DM at the time – nearly five times the cost of a standard 2WD Double Cab – and the list of options included leather upholstery, gun holders, gun cabinet in the locker bed, single seats in the rear and even a fridge.

Unsurprisingly perhaps, given the cost and limited market, the vehicle was not a big seller.

Of about 43,500 Syncro models built, only 2,138 featured the 16-inch optional package, of which only a very small number were Double Cabs converted as Jagdwagens.

The Jagdwagen featured here was built on 21 September 1988 and finished in Escorial Green. It has the 112bhp DJ petrol engine and fitted options include the 16-inch off-road

ABOVE: The base package included the full external roll cage and front-mounted winch.

package, opening front vent windows, power steering, dual diff locks, full Jagdwagen roll cage, Thiry front winch and cover, spare wheel sited on the rear cab wall, cover for cargo bed with inner frame work, rear sliders, walk-through cab, rectangular headlamps, tachometer and heated rear window. Now owned by Volkswagen enthusiast Lars Neuffer, it was discovered when a friend of a friend purchased a large forest area complete with house. Part of the deal included this Jagdwagen, which he had no use for. It still bore muddy signs of recent use and had clearly been looked after and used as intended, with only 65,000 kilometres (40,000 miles) on the clock.

The Jagdwagen optional equipment list included the following, with an additional note from Volkswagen that any special fittings or requirements could also be met.

Sixteen-inch wheels were used for vehicles that were specifically for regular off-road/rough terrain use, giving more ground clearance.

- Interior
  - Single seats in rear cabin instead of the standard bench seat
  - Leather upholstery and panels
  - Gamma radio with four speakers
  - Dash storage unit and cup holder
  - Rifle-mounting plates in cabin rear
  - Secure rifle box in the underbed locker area

- Leather-bound steering wheel
- 12V plug socket in cabin rear
- Deposit box at co-driver's door
- 'Diavia' air conditioning unit under the dashboard
- Coolbox (fridge) between rear seats.
- Exterior
  - Front bull bars
  - Roll cage and branch deflector
  - Holder for spare wheel at cabin rear wall
  - Holder for spare fuel can/tank at cabin rear wall
  - Spotlight mounted on the roll cage

- Heavy-duty (2.25 ton) rope hoist/winch for 2.25 ton load
- Winch cover for above
- Additional light front ('far beamer' 140mm diameter)
- Germer sunroof
- Double sound horn
- Cover for loading area (Cabriolet tarpaulin textile)
- Aluminium side gates
- Extra rear door
- Hardtop cab-height plastic cover for the load area.

LEFT: Truck mirrors have been added for better rear vision.

RIGHT: Plastic wheel arch flares were fitted to cover up where VW/Steyr had to modify the rear edge of the wheel arches to allow clearance for the larger diameter wheels and tyres.

SO 31 HEATING OIL DELIVERY TRUCK

From 1960 a Pick-Up specially equipped to deliver heating oil was available as SO 31. Converted by Schwelmer Eisenwerk, the oil tank mounted on the load bed had a capacity of 650 litres, with the oil delivered direct to the customer at home or work via a 30-metre hose and pump capable of delivering 85 litres per minute.

1961 VW brochure.

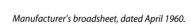

Manufacturer's broadsheet, dated April 1960.

The 1962 brochure still used photographs of 1960 Pick-Up models (note the round rear lights).

LEFT AND BELOW: This version of SO 31 was spotted in Vienna in 1981, still fully functional and working for a living delivering oil.

EA 489: THE VOLKSWAGEN MULI

The Muli was designed to be a low-cost vehicle, assembled from Volkswagen-supplied and locally made components.

This unusual looking Pick-Up, designated EA 489 (Entwicklungs-Auftrag – Development Order), was designed in the early 1970s by Volkswagen to meet potential markets in developing and Third World countries. Nicknamed 'Muli' (Mule), Volkswagen supplied the engine, transmission, front axle and steering gear along with detailed plans for producing and assembling sheet metal panels (with no pressed mouldings) for the cab and front end. The wood frame load-carrying section was assembled on the rear chassis frame and could also be fitted with benches for people transport. The engine was a 1.6-litre Beetle motor designed to run on low octane fuel, and the aim was for local economies to make and assemble the vehicles themselves at low cost, and thus offer them for sale at low prices. However, it seems that functionality suppressed design, and the local populace preferred to buy cheap Japanese Pick-Up imports instead, so the idea never really caught on. Apart from the production prototypes, only about 2,600 were built as CKD (Completely Knocked Down) kits in Hanover and approximately 3,600 more in Mexico from 1975 to 1979, some with a bay window front.

Several local variants of the Muli were also built: in Latin America a strange truck called Hormiga (ant), in Indonesia a T2 Kombi version called Mitra, and in Finland the Teijo. Another strange version, featuring a front motor and front wheel drive arrangement,

Plans were supplied for a sheet metal construction cab with no pressed mouldings.

The wood frame load-carrying section was assembled on the rear chassis frame and could also be fitted with benches for people transport.

was a bay window front Pick-Up, which carried the EA 489 script badge. It was produced for the home market by a Turkish importer in the mid 1970s.

Around two to three hundred of these are thought to have been built, using T2 styling and front panel and smooth cab doors.

BELOW AND RIGHT: Turkish-built variants of the EA 489 featured a front-mounted motor and front-wheel drive arrangement using a T2 cab.

catastrophe and disaster buses

KATASTROPHENSCHUTZWAGEN

To complement emergency service response to major road accidents or natural disasters such as flooding, a specially equipped Kombi, known as the Katastrophenschutzwagen, or Disaster Van, was often attached to fire stations, especially in rural areas. Crewed and fully equipped for six volunteer fire fighters, it was a rapid response unit designed to be deployed in the

event of a major emergency requiring manpower as well as specialist equipment. As well as field stretchers and first aid boxes the vehicle also carried ladders, torches, fire extinguishers, cones, spades and axes. The vehicle was fitted with a full-length roof rack, blue flashing light and Bosch sirens, an emergency mirror stalk spotlight and a pole-mounted detachable spotlight on the front panel. All Katastrophenschutzwagen featured 12V electrics and Eberspächer heater.

The 1962 Katastrophenschutzwagen shown here was one of thirty-eight supplied to the Rheinland-Pfalz Katastrophenschutz, as the area has several main rivers and is subject to flooding. It was deployed in Bernkastel-Kues on the River Mosel and used until 1991, when it became one of the

first vehicles acquired by Bulli Kartei for their mobile museum. All its original equipment was intact and complete.

1960 STRAHLENMESSWAGEN RADIOACTIVITY MONITORING BUS

This specially converted bus was built for the Red Cross in the Odenwald area, specifically to independently monitor levels of air-borne radioactivity in the event of an accident at the nearby nuclear power plant. It is a Microbus, built in November 1960 and finished in Ivory, with factory-fitted Eberspächer heater, tow bar, electric fresh air fans, and the larger oil bath air cleaner. Other emergency equipment includes blue flashing light, mirror spotlight and fog lamps. Air intake was from specially designed units on the front and the roof, and was fed to analysing equipment inside the bus. The inside was kitted out as a field lab with gauges, monitors and hi-tech instruments enabling tests to give readings there and then; radio–telephone links kept lines of communication open and secure. A portable generator meant the vehicle was self reliant for powering all the scientific equipment, and the mobility of the van meant it could quickly move to give a wider picture if needed. A PA system, with roof loudspeaker, was fitted so that the public could be quickly informed of any potential danger.

The Strahlenmesswagen is still in near-perfect condition with all its equipment intact and functional. The only time it ever saw real use was after the meltdown at the Chernobyl nuclear reactor in 1986, when Europe was keeping a very concerned and close eye on the radioactivity released into the atmosphere and closely monitoring its drift. Now in the hands of the Heppenheim Red Cross old timer friends, it is brought out for display at special events.

Air intake was from specially designed units on the front and the roof, and was fed to analysing equipment inside the bus.

A PA system, with roof loudspeaker, was fitted so that the public could be quickly informed of any potential danger.

The inside was kitted out as a field lab with gauges, monitors and hi-tech instruments enabling tests to give readings there and then.

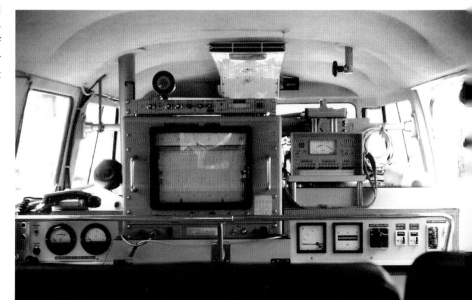

Bundesverwaltungsamt Zentralstelle für Zivilschutz	**T y p e n b l a t t** **Funkkraftwagen**	**FuKW 78**
Referat V A 2		Stückzahl: **182**

Bezeichnung des Fahrzeugs: **So.Kfz. Zivilschutz, Funkwagen**		
Fahrzeugtyp: **VW-Kombi, Typ 21** Größenklasse: **M 1**	Hersteller: **Volkswagen AG** BA-Nr.:　**1147/74, 1129/76, 1036/77,** 　　　　　**1179/77**	Forderung an den Kraftfahrer: **Klasse 3** später **Klasse B**

1977 Factory data sheet for the FuKW 78 Radio Van.

A radio unit and mobile command centre on show at Vanfest.

NUCLEAR DISASTER/CRISIS CONTROL BUSES

In the late 1970s the threat of war/ nuclear war still dominated European politics and in West Germany the Iron Curtain was the front line. Unbeknown to the general public, the German Government commissioned some special Katastrophenschutzwagen, which were designed specifically to act as mobile command and radio centres in the event of a major catastrophe, including the nuclear war scenario. Built in 1978 by Brunn of Bonn, they were usually deployed in pairs at strategic fire stations and fully equipped with various self-contained radio communication systems in order to act as coordination units. They were kept serviced and ready for use, but fortunately never saw active service and the general public were not aware of their purpose or existence! There were two versions – an operational mobile command vehicle (Führungskraftwagen) and a radio unit (Funkkraftwagen).

Both versions had Bosch sirens and flashing blue light and were equipped with a 220V input, a generator, twin batteries (three-way power for the radio set), two field telephones, a radio mast, a battery charger, an Eberspächer petrol heater and a 2-litre engine. Standard equipment included first aid box, winch, stepladder, axes, steel tow ropes and NATO convoy flags. Finished in Civil Service Orange, they carried logos of the fire station where they were based as well as their individual radio call signs. Distinctive body modifications included a rear step and aerial mounting point on the rear bumper, a flared finger lip on the rear tailgate, earth bonding point and a generator power cable access flap and aerial sockets on the rear nearside panels.

FuKW: MOBILE RADIO UNIT (FUNKKRAFTWAGEN)

Basically a Radio Van, manned by a radio platoon, the Funkkraftwagen was based on a walk-through Panel Van with an unusual part side window arrangement, sometimes called a half panel van (factory option M756), and a windowless tailgate. One hundred and eighty-two of these were built and commissioned in 1978, hence the designation FuKW 78.

FuKW 78

The mobile Radio Unit was manned by a crew of three and had full FM transceiver equipment as well as field telephones and landline access. A large radio antenna was mounted on the rear bumper and a self-contained generator and cabling were stored above the engine compartment. Because powerful radio equipment was carried, a half windowed Panel Van (M756) and solid rear tailgate was used, with the same body modifications and external specs as described above. The inside was kitted out as an office with telephone and handsets on a bench running along the side-wall. A shelved filing cupboard featured a pullout extension leaf that could be used from the rear bench seat.

The Funkkraftwagen was based on a walk-through Panel Van with an unusual part side window arrangement, sometimes called a half panel van.

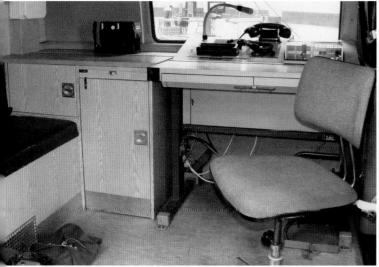

The inside was kitted out as an office with telephone and handsets on a bench running along the sidewall.

1978 Radio Unit (Funkkraftwagen).

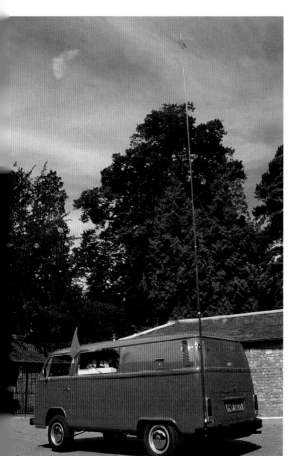

ABOVE: Convoy flag mountings were sited on each side.

LEFT: A large radio antenna was mounted on the rear bumper. Apart from the windowless rear tailgate the same body modifications and external specs as for the command version applied.

ABOVE: A small access flap for the generator cables was cut into the rear nearside.

FüKW: MOBILE COMMAND CONTROL (FÜHRUNGSKRAFTWAGEN)

Only one hundred and twelve FüKW-TEL 80 were built. Its function was a mobile telecommunications unit, forming part of the leadership group TEL (Technische Einsatzleitung – Technical Action Management – 80 refers to year of commission, in this case 1980). Based on a Kombi bulkhead model, the FüKW-TEL 80 version featured field telephones, radio transmitter and shortwave radio system powered from the generator stored in the rear. The interior was a functional office with twin benches, Perspex-topped map table with hinged extension flap, additional radio transmitters and receivers

1980 Operational mobile command vehicle (Führungskraftwagen).

The original first aid kit, sited under the dash.

Although walk-through models, bulkhead bench seating was installed.

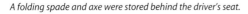

A folding spade and axe were stored behind the driver's seat.

The fold-down map table has a removable Perspex top and extension flap.

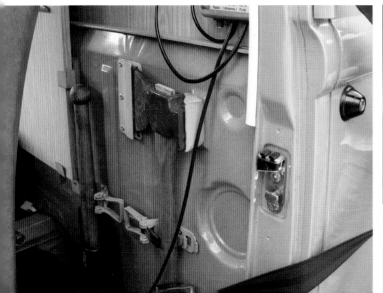

(which are operational outside the unit) and an inside rear view mirror and a heated rear window.

The interior was quite basic and geared totally to its use as a self-contained mobile command centre. The twin benches have storage under, with open shelving at the end of the bulkhead seat, and the map table has a removable Perspex top and extension flap. Cupboards above the back of the rear seat house more radio equipment and transmitters, while the cab has a dash-mounted field telephone, a map light on flexible stalk and another storage box unit between the cab seats as well as the original first aid kit sited under the dash.

The cab has a dash-mounted field telephone, a map light on flexible stalk and another storage box unit between the cab seats.

FüKW-TEL 80

Now owned by John Renshaw, the Disaster Van featured here is one of the very few to have survived that still has most of its original fittings. It went into service in 1980 and was based at Bersenbruck fire station in the Osnabrück region. Original equipment still with the bus includes snow chains, radio control box, dash telephone handset, convoy flags, leather document pouches, folding spade and axe, generator and radio equipment. Its original 18-64 call sign ID number is carried on the windscreen.

RIGHT: *A portable folding ladder and generator were stored above the engine compartment.*

RIGHT: *Distinctive body modifications included a rear step and aerial mounting point on the rear bumper, a flared finger lip on the rear tailgate, earth bonding point and a generator power cable access flap and aerial sockets on the rear nearside panels.*

ABC-Erkundungskraftwagen (ABC-ErkKW) was basically a stock eight-seater Kombi used as a personnel transport and reconnaissance vehicle.

T3 KATASTROPHENSCHUTZWAGEN

Two versions of Disaster Vans were built on the T3 base. They were mainly attached to fire stations to attend major incidents. The half panel van versions were designated Führungskraftwagens (FüKW-TEL 81 and FüKW-TEL 85) acting as radio command and coordination units and kitted out much like the FüKW-TEL 80s described above. The windowed version, ABC-Erkundungskraftwagen (ABC-ErkKW), was basically a stock eight-seater Kombi used as a personnel transport and reconnaissance vehicle.

Some further Disaster Control Buses were built on the T3 base including a Syncro version, but the changing world was marked by the fall of the Berlin Wall and subsequent re-unification of Germany.

In the 1990s the Disaster Control units were decommissioned and either mothballed or taken over for general use by fire stations, often repainted in red. They began to appear for sale around 2000 and were quickly snapped up by buyers. They were clean, low-mileage, well-maintained vehicles. Most had been stripped of all interior fittings and many have since been converted into Campers.

The half panel van versions were designated Führungskraftwagen (FüKW-TEL 81 and FüKW-TEL 85) and acted as radio command and coordination units.

12

Carlux mini coach

ABOVE: Designed as a tourist coach for sightseeing, the Carlux features a large one-piece front screen, long side windows, large rear corner windows and six large Plexiglas roof windows, as well as a new single full-width passenger door.

RIGHT: The new windscreen was flush to the roof and a pre-1955 Behr air scoop was fitted for fresh air. Note the modified cab door tops with shaped side windows to accommodate the wrap-around windscreen.

In 1960 the coachbuilder Ernst Auwärter, based in Stuttgart, produced this version of a tourist mini-coach featuring a large one-piece front screen (a bay window!), long side windows and large corner windows. To maximize visibility for viewing scenic panoramas, a further six large Plexiglas roof windows were also fitted. The conversion involved removing the top section above the belt line and fabricating a complete new roof and window section. The new wrap-around windscreen was flush to the roof, so a Behr air scoop was fitted for ventilation. The cab door tops had to be modified to accommodate the new windscreen, and new shape side windows added. The twin cargo door was replaced by a new full-width single door, hinged at the front end, and the tailgate window had to be narrowed to allow for the new large corner windows. Clearly inspired by the Samba, the Carlux Mini Coach provided six (or seven) tourists with a more intimate experience, with excellent views all round, and was ideal for both mountainous regions and city tours. Limited numbers of these were built and only two or three are known to survive. The one shown here was built in 1961/62 and used in Switzerland.

The large corner windows meant the window section of the tailgate had to be narrowed. The half moon recess clearly dates the vehicle to 1961/62.

Unfortunately, this is the fate of most of the Carlux conversions.

ABOVE: Brazilian taxi.

Amongst the Brazil-only special body variants was a taxi with a unique twin side door arrangement, with doors on both sides hinged at the front and a central pillar.

Brazilian-built buses used an unusual mixture of discontinued Volkswagen parts and panels and locally sourced components, and are a fascinating blend of old and new, with Split models being produced until 1975, when the hybrid Bay/Split model was introduced. The reason for this mix was quite simple: as Volkswagen updated its models it donated the old presses, dies and moulds to VW Brazil. This, coupled with the use of locally sourced and manufactured components, explains why discontinued parts and panels are mixed with later body panels and parts on the Brazilian buses built until 1979. Apart from its own distinctive versions of standard models, VW Brazil also produced its own range of locally produced SO models and,

A 1960s brochure entitled Different Aspects of a Single Quality showed a full range of special body variants.

Different aspects of a single quality
Diversas apariencias de una unica calidad

It does not matter what kind of freight you have to carry. You have the simplest and most economical solution for that. The conception of the Volkswagen Light Commercial models is perfectly adaptable to any kind of special equipment that is required to solve your problem.

Volkswagen always has the apposite solution for any type of transportation, in an easy and economical way to serve better the needs of your business.
Do not forget that all of them are provided with the quality of the Volkswagen mechanic.

Remember this, in special when the time of solving your problem will come. Ask your General Importer and see how easy it is to adapt your Volkswagen Light Commercial as you want.

No importa la espécie de carga que Ud. tiene que transportar. Ud. tiene la solución más sencilla y la más económica. La concepción de la línea de Comerciales Ligeros Volkswagen es perfectamente adaptable a cualquier tipo de equipo especial que fuera necessario para solucionar su problema.

Volkswagen siempre tiene la solución adecuada para cualquier tipo de transporte, de una forma fácil y económica para servir mejor las necesidades de su negocio.

No se olvide que todos ellos estan provistos con la calidad de la mecanica Volkswagen.

Acuérdese de esto, sobre todo cuando venga la hora de resolver su problema. Consulte su Importador General y vea cuan fácil es adaptar su Comercial Ligero Volkswagen tal como Ud. desea.

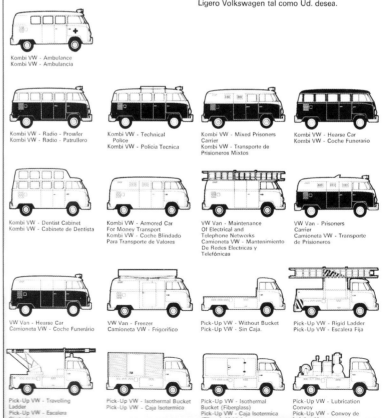

FROM TOP TO BOTTOM: Brazilian hearse.
Brazilian prisoner transport bus.
Brazilian mortuary vehicle.

in 1963, at the Sao Paulo Motor Fair, it exhibited its own Ambulance, Fire Truck, mobile dentist's bus with a high roof and additional windows, a mobile library and Refrigerated Transport vehicle. By 1967 the range had expanded to include Hearses, Mortuary vehicles, Prisoner Transport buses with cells, fixed and swivelling ladder trucks, telephone line maintenance vans, oil delivery Pick-Ups, Wide Bed Pick-Ups and police vehicles. Versions of these continued after 1975 using the hybrid T1/T2 model, which had a Split-style rear and a Bay Window front end. In 1997 a restyled Bay Window model with higher roof profile and mouldings on the lower cab door sections was introduced. The air cooled Transporters were phased out in 2005 when a new water-cooled model with front radiator grille went into production. The tradition of home-produced Special Bodies has continued into the restyled Brazilian Bays, as can be seen in the gallery overleaf.

carro funerário

A Kombi funerária é equipada com uma mesa de aço montada sôbre trilhos, e que desliza para fora do carro. Uma divisão metálica, com visor, separa o compartimento do motorista.
As janelas do compartimento de carga são fixas.
A pintura interna é na côr cinza, e a externa pode ser branca ou preta.

carro de presos

O Furgão VW para carro de presos é dividido em 3 compartimentos separados por chapas de aço reforçado: o compartimento do motorista, a divisão dos presos e um espaço reservado à instalação de rádio-comunicação. O compartimento de presos, por sua vez, é dividido em 2 celas completamente independentes e dotadas de grades reforçadas. Cada cela possui uma trava de segurança, acionada diretamente da cabina do motorista. O teto e o compartimento dos presos são dotados de respiradores. A pintura é em côr padrão polícia, com dizeres "Polícia", na frente e atrás.

mortuário

O Furgão VW adaptado para carro mortuário é dividido em 2 andares, por plataformas metálicas especiais, um com acesso pelas portas laterais, e o outro pela porta traseira. Cada andar contém duas urnas mortuárias, que deslizam sôbre roletes giratórios de aço. Uma divisão metálica separa hermeticamente a cabina do compartimento de transporte. A pintura é em côr padrão polícia, com os dizeres "Polícia", na frente e atrás.

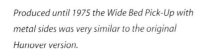
Produced until 1975 the Wide Bed Pick-Up with metal sides was very similar to the original Hanover version.

Brazilian special bodies

Box Delivery Vans based on Pick-Ups were very popular conversions.

One very unusual conversion was the mobile Dentist Van featuring a roof extension (looking remarkably like the top section of a bus) with large windows for increased light.

From 1997 the Brazilian models featured a higher profile roof and cab door mouldings amongst their refinements, as can be seen on this School Bus.

The Elma Chips delivery fleet featured Luton top conversions.

The Bay Brazilian Wide Bed Pick-Up had metal side gates that were made slightly higher by the addition of an open frame.

The Volkswagen has always been very popular with roadside fast food vendors and the latest water-cooled Bay-styled models have continued this tradition.

Brazilian emergency services also have continued to make extensive use of the locally built Transporter in its water-cooled version with the distinctive front radiator grille, as can be seen in the post-2005 versions below.

RIGHT: Wide Bed Cafe.

Post 1997 air-cooled enclosed Panel Van converted for selling fast food.

This street cafe features a pull out awning.

This shop conversion is one of the post-2005 water-cooled models, featuring a front mounted radiator.

Brazil's Emergency Services now use the latest water-cooled models for their fleet vehicles, as can be seen in these examples of a Police Kombi (above), Ambulance (left) and Fire Truck Panel Van (below). Apart from the distinctive front-mounted radiator grill (sporting the VW badge) note also the removable flashing light systems and the roll-up shutter door and carry bars on the fire truck.

1975 BRAZILIAN TAXI TYPE 201 DELUXE 6-DOOR KOMBI

With its rear corner windows the styling is borrowed from pre-1963 Deluxe Microbuses, though the base model is in fact a Kombi.

Of the many special body variants pro duced by the VW factory in Brazil, this six-door taxi is one of the more unusual and uncommon models.

The most distinctive, and notice-able, feature of this special model is the side door opening arrangement; instead of the usual side loading doors, there are twin opening doors, hinged at the front, on each side with a central pillar between them. (This C pillar is the same as used on double cabs.) Designated the 'Typo 201 Kombi Luxo com 6 portos' (Type 201 Deluxe 6-door Kombi) it featured opening doors on both sides, with side steps under for easier passenger access. This arrangement allowed room for eight passengers, and the doors on both sides made for easy access. The model number is also interesting as 201 is not a standard VW designation – VW Kombis were Type 23 and Microbuses Type 22. Type 201 was available from September 1960, and only as a special order; from 1960 to 1962 it is believed only about one hundred and ninety were actually built and, at most, a further couple of hundred from 1963 to 1975. The one featured here was built in February 1975, at the end of the Split (T1) production run, just before the T2 Fleetline models went into production.

With its rear corner windows it looks like a Samba, but is actually based on a Kombi not a Microbus. It has many of the recognizable hybrid features typical of Brazilian buses: the engine lid is the 1955–58 style, minus the central brake light, with its handle positioned slightly higher, and has a 1500 script badge; it features corner windows and a pre-1962-style Deluxe small tailgate with half moon recess

Probably the most distinctive feature of the Taxi is the unique side door opening arrangement of twin opening doors on each side, hinged at the front, with a central pillar between them.

above the T handle; the electrics are 12V; the side doors have pre-1955 Barndoor-style handles; the door hinges are the pre-1960-style high upper hinge position; door handles are the early pullout style; six pop-out windows (which have been replaced at some point on this example); post-1966 twin speed wipers; Bay Window style wiper and light knobs; a Brazilian-made speedometer; no heating and large 250mm brake drums. The engine is a 1500cc, 42bhp unit and has a cyclone air filter as standard, while the gearbox gear ratio is a max 100km/h (60mph) instead of 105km/h. Inside

The front hinged twin door arrangement allowed access to both rear and middle seat banks.

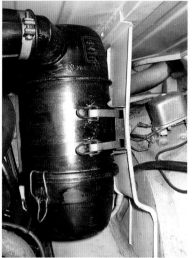

Note the full-width middle seat arrangement and the quilt pattern side panels.

there are three interior lights, extra grab handles for the passengers and ashtrays for each seating bank. Interior panels are black and feature a diamond stitch pattern. The dash grab handle is black, there are no rear window bars, the middle seat has a 1950s-style bar and the bumpers are pre-1966 slash end style. The rear bumper also has a special standing plate fitted between the over-riders. The front indicators and rear lights were manufactured locally and feature separate chrome rings around the lenses.

The first owner bought the bus new in 1975 and used it as a taxi for the next 29 years, before reluctantly parting with it in 2005, passing it on to German enthusiast Peter Valentin.

ABOVE RIGHT: A cyclone air filter was standard equipment for the Brazilian-built taxi.

RIGHT: The fuel gauge is one of many locally made components.

BELOW: The double doors allow passengers to alight simultaneously.

BELOW LEFT: . Side steps were fitted on both sides.

BELOW RIGHT: . Deluxe trim adds styling. Note the rain gutter protection above the cab doors.

police vehicles

ABOVE: This 1952 Unfallkommando shown in the 1955 brochure is set up to act as a mobile incident/interview room.

The first Transporter to be converted for use by the police services was built on a Kombi in 1950 for the Kiel Police Department. The Mannschafts Transportwagen (Crew Transport) featured a folding table and light attached to the front bulkhead, and a hinged flap-up dash table for the front passenger. An enclosed cell section in the rear was for carrying a prisoner and the side and rear windows were fitted with reinforced wire mesh.

The police were very quick to see the possibilities of the Transporter, and by the early 1950s Westfalia offered a Mobile Incident Room conversion, which developed to eventually become listed as SO 4, and then SO 3 for Bay Window models.

Also shown in the brochure is another 1952 version with roof platform featuring the newly available full-width dash option.

This archive picture shows a 1951 Unfallkommando (Mobile Incident vehicle) and its proud driver.

SO 4 POLICE ACCIDENT/ INCIDENT VEHICLE

Known as Unfallkommando (Police Accident Unit), SO 4 was a basic mobile incident room with the addition of a specially reinforced platform roof rack, with integral ladder and emergency lights. The original interiors for SO 4 were designed to be used for interviews and recording notes, with two facing benches round a table which could fold down against the sidewall, a single box seat, desk lamps, under storage and filing trays. The wood was all birch ply, as were the interior panels in the office area. The cab area also featured a folding dash table and leather document/map wallet on the passenger door, as well as a shortwave handset on the dash and shortwave radio equipment in the 'office' by the load door. A load-door-mounted toiletry cabinet complete with washbowl was usually part of the standard fitments. A unique feature was the special Westfalia roof rack fitted on the accident vehicles. Specially strengthened, this features a slide-out ladder to access a platform, which provided a perfect position for taking photographs at the scene of road traffic accidents. Additional flashing blue lights, PA loudspeakers and a pole-mounted spotlight could also be mounted on the rack.

The VW factory-prepared base model was a bulkhead Kombi painted in Police Green (Tannengrün/Fir Tree Green RAL 6009) with chrome hubcaps and fitted with optional equipment – M623 (shortwave radio equipment) and M160 (Bosch siren and blue flashing light) – as standard. Additional commonly fitted options included an Eberspächer heater (M119), fresh air fans (M121), sliding door (M169) and cab partition with sliding window (M529). Police workshops and garages also often made their own modifications and changes to base vehicles, including changes of use.

Staged photograph from the early 1960s shows an SO 4 and officers in action at an accident, recording details on the spot.

1952 Unfallkommando (accident unit) in action. The dark blue colour was used for Berlin police buses.

1960 Police unit used in Düsseldorf. A loudspeaker is mounted on the cab roof and the blue flashing light postioned on the mid-side. The cab/load areas have a windowed divider.

police vehicles

1966 SO 4

The 1966 example featured here has been restored to recreate an authentically styled SO 4 model, although it was originally used by the Heerespolizei (Swiss Military Police), which accounts for the lower gear ratio (M92) and limited slip diff (M220) factory-fitted options. Rescued in 2002 and restored by Michael Zierz, it has since been fitted with the correct and rare original period fittings including platform roof rack and ladder, radio handsets and shortwave equipment, dash table and leather map document pouch. An original late 1960s Westfalia Police interior has been refurbished and fitted, and original Westfalia rear cabinets from an early Bay Window Police Van have been added. As well as leisure use, the bus is also used for special displays and events, recreating the period. Genuine period police accessories such as a typewriter (with olive green keys), traffic police white trench coat and hats, flashing warning lights, emergency stretcher and original handbooks, documents and writing pads add to the effect.

Twin Bosch bumper sirens, painted badge hubcaps and handles, and Unfallkommando sign are period correct.

ABOVE: Flashing blue lights, PA loudspeakers and a pole-mounted spotlight are mounted on the roof rack.

BELOW: A specially strengthened Westfalia roof platform rack was fitted on the accident vehicles, which provided a perfect position for taking photographs at the scene of road traffic accidents.

ABOVE: To access the platform a slide-out ladder is stored under the roof rack. (Note: the Microbus seats seen in this picture were temporarily installed while the police interior was being restored.)

All the fittings are original period police equipment including radio handsets and shortwave equipment.

The cab area featured a folding dash table, leather document/map wallet on the passenger door and hand-held signalling disc.

The insides were lined with birch ply as on Westfalia's Campers. The rear cabinets are also Westfalia, but from an early T2 Police Van.

Period accessories such as the genuine police typewriter, shortwave handset, warning lights and traffic police hat and coat create an authentic SO 4 look.

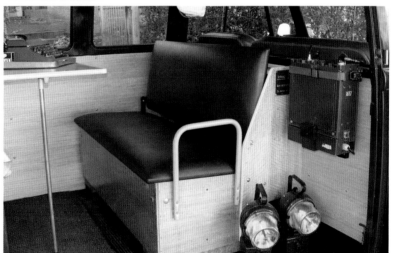

The office-style interior basically consisted of two facing benches and a table. Items such as lights and tools could be stored under the seats, and a stretcher under the bulkhead seat (note side access hole for it).

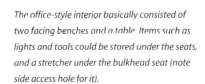

The CID Mobile Office Unit Kfz 57 had shelved desk drawers and more comfortable seating.

Kfz 52 was a Mobile Cinefilm Camera and Projection Unit.

Kfz SPECIAL CONVERSIONS

The German police made extensive use of the VW Bus across a whole spectrum of uses: for traffic control, accidents and emergencies, traffic education (with tape recorder PA system, loudspeakers, film and slide projectors and projection screens), radar speed checking, mobile forensic laboratories, CID units and even as a Black Maria (Prisoner Transport Bus) with two secure cells in the loading bay. To meet these needs, in 1964 Westfalia introduced variants on SO 4, each designed for a specific use. Prefixed Kfz (from Kraftfahrzeug, motor vehicle), these were:

Prisoner Transport (Kfz 58) featured a cell and seat for police escort.

- Kfz 52: Mobile Cinefilm Camera and Projection Unit, used to both record and film incidents and for publicity/ education.
- Kfz 53: Portable radar speed camera unit for setting up at the roadside.
- Kfz 54: Radar Van with built-in cameras in the front panel and a rear-facing unit used with the tailgate open.
- Kfz 57: CID Mobile Office Unit, usually with full-length roof rack and cover.
- Kfz 58: Prisoner Transport Wagon (Black Maria) with load area partitioned into cell and police escort room.

RADAR UNITS

Radar speed control vehicles were often modified by police garage workshops, or speciality garages, and radar equipment could be used as a freestanding roadside unit or could be fitted directly inside the vehicle. This was usually mounted in the area above the engine bay, or behind glass windows cut into the front panel as in the example opposite, but some conversions had an opening front hinged door.

1962 FRONT OPENING RADAR BUS

Only twenty T1 models with an opening front door were actually built. The one shown here was a 1962 Kombi delivered to the Frankfurt police, who modified it into a radar surveillance unit. This involved cutting the front panel to make a hinged front opening door. The dashboard had to be shortened to accommodate the opening front door and the new front screen is slightly smaller than standard so that a windshield frame could be fitted in the door. Each front screen has its own wiper motor, which runs independently at different speeds, although the same switch controls them.

The radar unit was mounted on rails; in transit it occupied the space normally used by the passenger and simply rolled forwards to use. This was much easier than freestanding systems, which needed to be set up at the roadside. The radar unit was manufactured by Multanova and offered

BELOW: *This early Bay Radar Bus was used in its original Neptune Blue to be unobtrusive. Converted in Germany it saw service with the Dutch police. It only had a driver's seat up front, as the passenger area was taken up with the radar equipment and sliding rails.*

state of the art surveillance since the equipment could distinguish between vehicles travelling side by side on the autobahn. The loading area was equipped as a mobile office with a desk running under the windows from where the radar unit was operated.

Extra electrical power to operate the radar unit was supplied by a system using three batteries and a twin generator set up, enabling power to be supplied at either 6V or 12V.

In 1982 it was taken to a scrap yard for crushing but was saved at the eleventh hour by Chris Christensen, who fully rebuilt the chassis and restored the bus over a period of seven years. It is now a fully equipped Camper featuring swivelling front seats.

This archive photograph of a T2 Radar Van was taken at a Police exhibition in Wöllstadt in 1971.

This 1972 Swiss Police Radar Van has the equipment mounted on slide-out rails at the rear of the vehicle.

1967: SO 3

From 1967 Westfalia offered the Unfall-kommando model on the new Bay Window base. Although almost identical to the SO 4 version, it now carried the special model code designation SO 3. As the Bay models were walk through, a metal partition was fitted between the cab and load area (M500), with the option of a sliding glass partition for the upper half (M523). Laminated windscreen and Eberspächer heater were now standard factory-fitted options, and the front bench became a single seat with cupboard next to it. A full range of accident/emergency control equipment such as reflective clothing, road signs and cones, flashing warning lamps and first aid kit was also carried. Such equipment was not factory fitted but added by the individual Police Departments where a unit was to be based.

1978 POLICE PA/LOUDSPEAKER VAN

Built in October 1978 this Police Van was converted as a Loudspeaker Van by F.X. Kogel and delivered to the Hamburg Police Riot Squad. It has a bank of five rotating loudspeakers mounted on the roof, extra windscreen washers with protective covers, and windows with special brackets for attaching wire mesh protection grilles. A side flap provides access for power hook up and the inside has a single and bench seat, table and microphones and PA equipment. In 2001 it was acquired by the German T2 Club and currently resides in the new Bulli Museum.

This period image showing traffic police and their SO 3 attending an accident was probably a publicity photograph.

The bank of five speakers rotates through 360 degrees.

Windscreen washer protection guards were fitted to ensure continued visibility for occupants.

Note the convoy flag mounting and the brackets for attaching wire mesh protection grilles.

145

UNDERCOVER AND SURVEILLANCE UNITS

1972 ANTI TERRORIST HIGH ROOF BUSES

As a direct result of the terrorist attack at the 1972 Munich Olympics, the German anti-terrorist unit GSG 9 (Grenzschutzgruppe 9; Border Guard Group 9) was created. Amongst the first vehicles put into commission by the unit were these two High Roof Buses, finished in light grey with white roofs.

The GSG 9 was a special anti-terrorism unit, comparable to the SAS, combining both intelligence gathering and armed rapid response.

As undercover units these buses were designed to resemble Ice Cream Vans and to blend into a typical German urban setting. Obviously much of the buses' usage, history and fittings is shrouded in secrecy, but they were converted and kitted out by Caterpillar/Zeppelin, delivered in December 1973 and first registered on 26 February 1974. The paperwork shows the owner to be the German Minister for Internal Affairs.

Both vans left the Hanover plant as walk-through models, fitted with the high roof and high sliding doors (M516). The M codes also show they were fitted with a windowless tailgate, Eberspächer heater, fog lights, laminated windscreen, fresh air fans and interior panelling fitted with rivets. Other interesting features include a signalling disc mounted inside the passenger's door, four working police sirens hidden under the front wheel arches, radio equipment and aerials, a generator, furniture (now removed), seating and cabinets, a curtain at walk through, fresh air fan in top of the roof, mounting pole for blue light and twin batteries. There are minor differences between the two vehicles; one is fully soundproofed inside with two flaps in the left side (possibly for surveillance) while the other has a grounding port and two windows in the top of the sliding door. These round windows seem to have been post factory modifications as they are engraved 'BUND', which means government item/property, and are the only ones like this

to have been found. This vehicle also has a twin interior light by the door. Decommissioned in November 1998, they are now owned by bus enthusiasts Roland Knauss and Gunther Mack.

As undercover units these buses were designed to resemble Ice Cream Vans and to blend into a typical German urban setting.

ABOVE AND BELOW: There are minor differences between the two vehicles; one is fully soundproofed inside with two flaps in the left side (possibly for surveillance) whilst the other has a two windows in the top of the sliding door.

1971 PANEL VAN SURVEILLANCE UNIT

What better way to blend unobtrusively into any German street than in a commercial, grey VW Delivery Van. This 1971 (1972 model) Panel Van was used by the Bielefeld Police Department as an undercover surveillance unit and was prepared by Westfalia. To preserve anonymity a removable tinted Perspex window fits on the tailgate and a black curtain screens off the load area. Factory-fitted options include cloth upholstery material exclusive to the German Bundespost and Police (M106), Eberspächer BN4 petrol heater, with outlet in the load/passenger compartment (M119), fibreboard interior roof panels (M503), opening quarter-lights (M507), shortwave radio equipment (M623), laminated windscreen glass (M089), lockable engine lid (M094), maximum axle loads and weights on the wheel arches (M065) and equipment group AO6 – a composite code for a full-width metal partition between the cab and load compartment (M500), fibreboard interior panel on the sliding door (M510), plus additional air vents in the rear side panels of the cargo compartment. Westfalia also installed a package that included installation of two dome-shaped ventilators in the roof (one to expel stale air and the other to draw in fresh air). To make long surveillance vigils slightly more comfortable, the interior was fitted with the Westfalia SO 72/7 basic camping equipment option, which consisted of a single seat behind the driver, a fold down on the side wall, rear bench seat, wardrobe by the sliding door, rear linen cupboard and a sink unit with side cupboard and flap-down shelves either side. The unit shown here was used up until 1995.

Converted and equipped by Westfalia, this 1971 Bay was designed to blend unobtrusively into any street.

The additional air vents and dome ventilators are the only external signs of a non-stock delivery van.

To make long surveillance vigils slightly more comfortable, the interior was fitted with the Westfalia SO 72/7 basic camping equipment.

T3 BEDO OBSERVATION AND INTELLIGENCE GATHERING VEHICLE

This specialist version is called a Bedo (Beweissicherungs- und Dokumentationsfahrzeug; evidence securing and documentation vehicle). It featured a reinforced roof rack with fold-up sides to make an enclosed observation platform which is accessed from inside the vehicle via a sliding roof section. Inside were two single seats on a bench, a single bulkhead seat and storage cabinets. Side windows were tinted and there was no rear window. It was used by the police to keep watch on, and photograph, individuals and incidents at gatherings such as football matches and demonstrations. The blue lights are detachable.

IN PLAIN CLOTHES

This innocuous looking T3 would have blended perfectly into any German street in the eighties and nineties. Finished in the commonly seen commercial blue, and looking like any nondescript minibus, it was perfect for undercover work. The only hint as to its real use is the roof stalks, on which could be mounted the flashing blue lights. As well as surveillance and undercover work it was also used as a personnel transport for the riot police, whose equipment was stored out of sight in the enclosed rear section.

T3, T4 AND T5 MODELS

The police continued to make extensive use of VW Transporters throughout the T3 and T4 generations, and the T5 now forms the core of their emergency response fleet.

BELOW LEFT AND RIGHT: This 1982 T3 was used by the Dutch police for transporting prisoners.

Finished in typical police livery, this T3 version was used as a tactical group vehicle and features rubber mesh safety dividers for the passenger area.

It also features front and rear flashing blue lights and a loudspeaker over the cab. Note the additional hazard warning flashers mounted at rear of roof.

BELOW: A fleet of riot police T4s on duty at the Munich football stadium.

RIGHT: A standard T4 'Streifenwagen' (patrol car) used by the Düsseldorf traffic police. Notice stop sign box mounted on the bonnet which shows 'stop' letters as mirror writing when lit, rear 'Mickey Mouse' ears' warning flashers on the roof and inside net protectors for safety reasons.

BELOW: This line up outside the VW Commercial Customer Centre in Hanover shows a fleet of Immigration Control T5s, each with only a single window in the sliding door side.

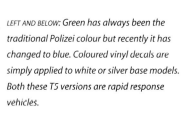

LEFT AND BELOW: Green has always been the traditional Polizei colour but recently it has changed to blue. Coloured vinyl decals are simply applied to white or silver base models. Both these T5 versions are rapid response vehicles.

A tiny, hardly visible, camera, is often mounted on the rear view mirror to record both speed and pursuit information during chases.

The T5 is now an integral part of the Police fleet, mainly as a rapid response or chase vehicle but also as personnel transport. Note the additional blue flashing lights built into the radiator grille of the Multivan pictured here and the bonnet mounted illuminated stop sign.

school buses

ABOVE: This picture was taken in the 1990s at a primary school in Tipton, West Midlands and was inspired by an early VW publicity image. Daisy, the 1962 23 window Samba shown, has an original Devon interior, not a Microbus as on the original.

The VW Microbus was ideal for ferrying children around, especially in rural areas. Mostly standard production line Microbus and Deluxe versions were used, and initial interest in the potential was boosted by the purpose demonstration model built in 1955.

1955 PROTOTYPE SCHOOL BUS

This Dove Blue Kombi School Bus was one of the first of the brand new post-Barndoor models. It was built in March 1955, on the Wolfsburg production line, as a prototype/demonstrator specifically for the American market, promoting the Kombi's people- and load-carrying possibilities. It featured the new front flashers, which were standard on USA models from 1955 but not on European models until 1960, and also the beltline single white pinstripe used on Kombis from 1952 to 1957/58. It had the Kombi walk-through option (M80) with a double middle seat, fitted side step, single fold-down 'jump' seat on the bulkhead, large grab handle, passenger

Special brackets on the gutter and access for wiring through the roof allowed the front and rear roof mounted signboards, with warning flashers, to be easily installed or removed.

CENTRE: The mounting points for the signboards and wiring access can be seen on this picture showing the signboards removed.

door safety restraint and extra hazard flashers on the rear. The whole rear section was painted yellow, as on all American School Buses, with black for the rear beltline. Special brackets on the gutter and access for wiring through the roof allowed the front and rear roof-mounted signboards, with warning flashers, to be easily installed or removed, showing the Kombi's versatility.

It was used for a few years in the USA by both a kindergarten and a primary school, resulting in increased sales of standard Kombis and Microbuses to children's homes, schools, parish communities and so on, where the model's size and versatility proved ideal. Having done its promotional job, it was then shipped back to Wolfsburg where it lay forgotten in the basement of the factory. In the early 1980s the School Bus went into the museum's store, dust-covered windows obscuring the roof signs stored inside, so no-one realized its rarity or significance and considered it to be just an uninteresting, ordinary Dove Blue Kombi with a strange yellow rear! A Bulli enthusiast discovered it there in the mid 1990s and rescued it. He pieced together the true background to the bus and for several years it was part of Bulli-Kartei's Mobile Museum, before being sold to a collector in the USA.

BELOW LEFT: The model featured a double middle seat, fitted side step, single fold-down 'jump' seat on the bulkhead, large grab handle and passenger door safety restraint. BELOW RIGHT: The whole rear section was painted yellow, as on all American School Buses, and extra hazard flashers fitted.

rail buses (Draisine)

Named after the inventor Karl Drais, Draisine were originally simple hand-operated trolley vehicles, designed to run on rail tracks to move equipment and workers onto site as well as for close inspection of track condition. In 1952/53, motorized versions, powered initially by Volkswagen's 22bhp industrial motor, and from 1953 a 28bhp version, were built and used by the German rail network, Deutsche Bundesbahn. These first versions were designated Klv 11 (abbreviated from Kleinwagen mit Verbrennungsmotor; small wagon with combustion engine).

They proved so useful and reliable that in early 1955 the Deutsche Bundesbahn commissioned a fleet of thirty Kombis, chassis numbers 20-5001 to 20-5031, for special conversion to run on rail tracks as Draisine, but which would be capable of carrying larger loads and/or a maintenance gang. Designated Klv 20, they were designed

and built by the railway Karosseriebau firms of Beilhack in Rosenheim and WMD Waggonfabrik in Donauwörth, which built fifteen each.

Using fixed axles and specially adapted wheels, lined with rubber to increase traction, only forward travel was normally used, with a maximum speed of 70km/h (45mph). Reverse gear was used for shunting. The standard drum brakes were retained but with a dual circuit system. As the bus runs on the railway track there is no steering wheel in the cab, and a new speedometer, calibrated to the non-standard wheels, was fitted next to the instrument pod. To change direction a hand-operated hydraulic pump lowered a steel frame down between the rail tracks and raised the bus up. When the wheels had cleared the tracks, the vehicle was then rotated manually; a tricky operation as the vehicle had to be kept level and balanced!

A large side footplate ran under the cargo doors and passenger cab door and one version shows a cab step on the driver's side and an extended platform with standing plate at the rear, which were probably later additions. A single, large, circular red rear light was fitted on the right-hand rear corner and a circular headlight on each front roof corner or on the outside edge of the window frame. The original bus headlights and rear lights were usually painted over or removed and the housing filled, although some versions have the original headlights and glass left in place. The Draisine were finished in Purple Red (RAL 3004) with a silver roof and silver swage line, which extended to the V shape on the front panel; the Beilhack versions also had a small three-dimensional Beilhack badge on each body side. Classed as Bahnamtsdraisine (BA Rail Buses), all versions carried stickers on both cab

Swiss Rail Buses were known as Tower Wagons. Based on Panel Vans they featured a special reinforced roof rack to which a ladder was fitted for the inspection and repair of overhead power cables.

doors showing the Klv number and technical information.

Used mainly on secondary rail tracks, they saw extensive use for building, signal and track inspection, as well as for ferrying loads and work crews. Most were decommissioned in the early 1970s when all the secondary lines were shut down. However, Klv 20-5011 remained in service until 1987 and Klv 20-5012 remained in use in Kaiserslautern until 1997.

While in service they were maintained by the Bremen Railworks Factory, who also carried out modifications such as an additional rear platform and tool holders for the front bumper. Although most of the Rail Buses were scrapped at the Bremen works, around a dozen still survive, mostly in museums, such as the blue-painted version shown here (a later

RIGHT: This version currently resides in the Berlin Museum of Transport. Over time it received many minor modifications such as cab step and tool holders mounted on the front of the bumper as well as the blue paint colour.

BELOW RIGHT: Other modifications include the rear standing platform.

BELOW: A large side footplate ran under the cargo doors and passenger cab door. The roof-mounted grab handle is another later addition.

colour change), which is housed in the Berlin Museum of Transport. There is also a fully restored working version, owned by the Hessencourier Rail Club in Kassel, which is regularly taken out for exhibition and can even be rented out for a very different 'driving' experience.

Rail Buses were also used by the Swiss railway service, which, in 1956, commissioned the Swiss firm Condor to build eight Draisine, numbered as Dm 3681–3688. These were very different from the Klv versions in that they used Panel Vans (post-Barndoor with the small engine lid) as the base model and were powered by the Porsche 365 engine. Painted in Coral Red (RAL 3016) and known as Tower Wagons, they featured a special reinforced roof rack onto which a ladder was fitted for the inspection and repair of overhead power cables. All were taken out of use in 1984 and scrapped.

Klv 20-5003 was built by Beilhack. The DB on the front stands for Deutsche Bundesbahn (German railway).

BELOW RIGHT: To change direction a hand-operated hydraulic pump lowered a steel frame down between the rail tracks, which raised the bus up off the track so it could be manually rotated. Note the Beilhack badge on the side.

BELOW LEFT: This archive picture of a Waggonfabrik version Klv 20-5004 dates from the late 1950s.

KLV 20-5028

The restoration project featured here is Klv 5028. Following its decommission, it was sold to the Bremervoerde-Osterholzer Railway, who modified it for use as a construction vehicle. It was rescued by rail enthusiast and Bulli Kartei member Sven Thomsen in 1995, who set about restoring it for display at special events such as Techno Classica. As well as restoring the undercarriage, he also rebuilt the hydraulic turning frame, and fitted the correct style of pressed bumpers, before repainting it in the original colours of Purple Red and Silver. Currently a full restoration is planned for this vehicle.

BELOW: The original headlights were left in place (or removed and the housing filled) and simply painted over. New circular spotlights were mounted on the front.

Bumpers and wheels were painted black.

The rear lights were also painted over and a large red circular rear light added.

The front lights on this version were mounted on each front roof corner, instead of the outside of the cab window frame.

ABOVE: The redundant steering wheel and gear were removed during conversion. It must have been very strange driving with no steering wheel! (The cab bench seat has been removed for restoration purposes.)

LEFT: All the instruments were also removed and replaced with a km/h speedometer with integral clock, which was calibrated to the non-standard wheels.

BELOW LEFT: Specially adapted wheels were lined with rubber to increase traction. The hand pump to operate the turning frame was sited by the front wheel.

BELOW RIGHT: The supporting frame for turning the vehicle can be seen slung under the chassis.

SO 19 display/ exhibition models

ABOVE: The 1955 sales brochure showed this
example of a 1951/52 display model used by
Gesamtverband der Leinenindustrie in Bielefeld
(General Federation of the Linen Industries).

As well as Delivery Vans or Mobile Shops, businesses also used a special body conversion featuring large glass side windows, in various arrangements, to exhibit or display goods. The first display conversion was described in the July 1951 VW Information, and the 1955 Special Interiors brochure featured a 1951 display bus with twin full-length display windows. A 1953 photograph from the Westfalia factory at Wiedenbrück shows a prototype model with one large side window.

The standard SO 19 designated version, produced from 1956 by the Freudenau Karosseriefabrik of Bielefeld, was based on a Panel Van and featured nine large windows: two large rectangular windows cut into the cargo doors and opposite sidewall, two more square-shaped windows behind on

This archive 1951 photograph shows a Panel Van with three large display windows on one side.

each side, and a large square window in the tailgate. Various arrangements of large windows could be fitted according to customer requirements, from a mix of large and small or single window taking up most of one side to a hinged version that opened like a sales flap.

This 1951/52 Kombi was used to demonstrate gas cookers shown in the 1955 brochure.

Taken at the Westfalia works, this photograph shows a 1953 prototype exhibition model featuring a large side window.

SO 19 display/exhibition models

BELOW LEFT: Artist's impression of how a Pick-Up could be used to promote building savings agreements. Note the cooling vents and slightly rounded rear side with a modified engine lid!

BELOW RIGHT: This Westfalia factory blueprint, dated 1957, shows details of a Kofferaufbau (Pick-Up with enclosed box container) with two large side windows and twin rear door windows, designed as an exhibition or display bus, or possibly for use as a hearse. None are known to have been built.

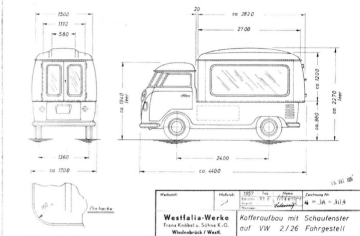

1957 SWEDISH SO 19

Originally used by a Swedish vacuum cleaner manufacturer to promote its products. Built in 1957 and originally finished in Dove Blue, it features a large glass window on one side and an unusual arrangement of long window in one cargo door and additional long window on the rear side panel. Original signwriting on cab doors and roof can still just be seen and there is also an external battery-charging socket on the rear corner.

ABOVE: The brochure also had this image of a mobile bathroom exhibition bus.

LEFT: These images of exhibition buses being used to promote sewing machines in Europe and Asia were reproduced in a 1962 brochure.

159

fire trucks (Feuerwehr)

ABOVE: 1956 Magirus Deutz conversion in original paint and signwriting.

As described on page 13, the November 1951 edition of *VW Information* carried information about the first Panel Van to be converted and kitted out as a Fire Truck by the firm Magirus Deutz. This featured a new single window on each side, roof rack and spotlight, and carried a full mobile pump unit, hoses and equipment. The VW Transporter was an ideal size for the smaller voluntary fire stations and factories, and demand for such a versatile workhorse was such that in 1952 Volkswagen introduced its own factory-prepared Fire Truck Panel Van with the designation 21F, fitted with a VW industrial motor powered water pump and fire fighting equipment. Revised model codes in 1959 saw this designation dropped and M codes, often grouped as a bundle, were used to identify a vehicle prepared for Fire Truck use. Emergency vehicle coachbuilders such as Magirus Deutz, Meyer-Hagen and Bachert continued to offer their own versions and also specialized in fire service conversions such as swivel ladder trucks, dry foam trucks, personnel vehicles and heavy-duty pump vehicles.

ABOVE: Magirus Deutz carried out the first VW Fire Truck conversion around October 1951, featuring a single window on each side, full-length roof rack and spotlight, and full mobile pump unit. This version dates from early 1952 (note longer upper cooling vents).

1956 MAGIRUS DEUTZ FIRE TRUCK

This 1956 fully equipped Fire Truck, complete with operational water pump, was built in October 1956 on chassis number 210 068. It was imported by Swiss importer AMAG as a Panel Van in Fire Truck Red and delivered to the Swiss branch of Magirus Deutz on 5 December who converted it and delivered it to Fritz Landolt AG textile works in Näfels on 20 December, for use as the factory fire truck. It was decommissioned in October 1994 with just 14,500 kilometres (9,000 miles) on the clock. In 1965 it was updated with flashers to comply with Swiss regulations, but apart from that it is completely unrestored and unwelded and still has most of the original paint. It even has the original service books for the van and pump as well as the original operator's manuals. As can be seen in the photos, the VW motor-powered water pump still works perfectly. After two UK owners, the truck was bought by Gary Collis in Australia, who owns a VW restoration business. He plans to put original-style lights back on and couple it to a fire trailer with a 25bhp auxiliary fire pump.

Note the maker's badge on the front.

In action at Vanfest in the late 1990s.

The original VW industrial pump motor and fittings are all still intact.

The Mannschaftswagen was a Kombi-based version designed for personnel transport and fitted with shortwave radio.

tailgate, door catches for side doors (to stop them from shutting in the wind), folding 'jump' seat mounted on the bulkhead, external battery charger socket DIN 14 690 and plastic document holder with lubrication chart. Also included was heating in the cargo bay (M141), laminated window glass (M90) and blue flashing light and Bosch double sirens (M160). Mud and snow tyres (M101) could also be specified.

STANDARD FIRE TRUCK EQUIPMENT

- blue light on roof and sirens (M160)
- portable pump TS 8/8 with VW industrial motor
- axes (3)
- rechargeable torch
- three-colour signal torches (3)
- red warning lamps (2)
- pair of asbestos gloves
- set of tools, spares and accessories
- long spade
- 700mm crowbar
- grappling hooks (3)
- 20m rope (3)
- hose mounts (3)
- bucket (2)
- sack
- 5m hose and pipe with A10 fitting
- small medical kit
- 5m tow rope
- ball of twine (2m × 8mm)
- canvas bag with tools
- red hazard signs (2)
- red and white hazard flags (2)
- hose cabinets and straps
- fire extinguisher
- spanners for ABC connectors (3)
- hydrant spanners (wrenches) (2)

TSF-T AND LLF

The designation TSF (T), Tragkraft-spritzenfahrzeug (Trupp) – mobile pump vehicle – was used for Panel Van Fire Trucks and was designed to carry a crew, fire equipment, hoses and a VW industrial engine powered water pump. Its basic crew was three and there was an optional folding seat on the bulkhead. As well as water pump and hoses, a full range of emergency and fire-fighting equipment, obtained from specialist fire-fighting manufacturers, was carried.

Light-duty vehicles with full equipment but sometimes without the water pump were designated LLF (Leichtlöschfahrzeug) and included Pick-Ups and Double Cabs, a Kombi-based version designed for personnel transport and fitted with short-wave radio called Mannschaftswagen, and a Kombi carrying a crew of nine with mobile pump unit on a trailer.

FIRE TRUCK SPECIFICATIONS

The standard Fire Truck was factory fitted with the M140 package, which consisted of Fire Truck Red paint (RAL3000/SK 688), chrome hubcaps, black wheels and bumpers (RAL9005), tyre pressures painted in white above wheel arches, interior panels on side doors, non-lockable side doors and

One tactical unit version used a Kombi (carrying up to nine fire fighters) with a mobile pump unit mounted on a trailer.

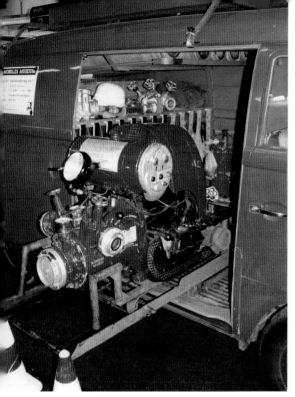

This original condition 1959 TSF-T (Mobile Pump Unit) also has the optional mud and snow tyres, Fire Truck small roof rack and pole-mounted front spotlight.

For ease of use the pump unit was mounted on a frame that slid out on runners.

- 1.6m suction hoses (5)
- 5m hose
- 20m hoses (6)
- 15m hoses (12)
- hose connectors, pipes and adaptors with B, C and Y fittings.

BAY WINDOW FIRE TRUCKS

This same specification continued for the Bay Window models, but a distinctive body modification was the re-positioning of the front bumper, raising it for better ground clearance. As for the T1, the base models were the Mobile Pump Unit and the Personnel Carrier, and a new version, the Commando Kombi (Kommandowagen), which had the interior arranged with seating, a table and radio telephones to act as a mobile office/communications centre. Ambulances painted in fire service livery were also often attached to larger stations for rapid response to accidents.

THE END OF THE MOBILE PUMP VERSIONS

By the time of the T3, the need for more sophisticated fire trucks capable of dealing with larger scale emergencies, coupled with re-organization of more integrated emergency services, marked the end of the Fire Truck

Hoses, connectors and fittings as well as fire extinguishers, ropes, axes, torches, first aid kit and so on were all stored inside.

mobile pump unit role, though factories and rural areas still used such vehicles. Instead the Transporter developed a key role as rapid response and coordination vehicle.

The gallery that follows shows just some of the many, varied types of Fire Truck conversion across five generations, making them probably Volkswagen's most successful specialized model.

RIGHT: *For Bay Window models the front bumper was repositioned slightly higher to give better ground clearance.*

fire trucks (Feuerwehr)

1962 DOUBLE CAB
FIRE/LADDER TRUCK

This model is unusual in that it has a swivel ladder rig fitted to a Double Cab, something prohibited in Germany due to weight restrictions. Built 16 March 1962 on chassis number 303 092 101 160, it was finished in Ruby Red and ordered by the South Tyrolean village Laas/Lasa in the Vinschgau region of the Italian Alps. It had the usual Fire Truck options of tow bar, Bosch sirens and blue emergency light and, as it was to be used in mountainous areas, it was also fitted with the lower ratio gears and mud and snow tyres as well as the Italian-spec side flashers. A Meyer-Hagen 10-metre wooden Ladder Truck conversion has been fitted to the load bed, making this the only T1 Double Cab Ladder Truck known. This version is mounted on a fully removable frame, which includes a swivel plate, and simply unbolts to remove from the bed, so the truck can function as a normal crew cab if required. The stabilizing feet on a rein-forced rear bumper, as normally found on ladder trucks, have not been fitted; another German market requirement clearly not necessary in Italy! A detach-able spotlight with a long power cable is mounted on the rear of the cab, allowing it to be fitted to the truck or hand held and a hand pump fire extinguisher with hose is also sited here. The Doka (Double Cab) saw only limited use in its time, spending the majority of its time parked in the fire station, and has only 20,000 kilometres (12,500 miles) on the clock. It was used for the Voluntary Fire Department Service and was finally retired from duty in early 1995. Now forming part of Micheal Zierz's bus collection, and still sporting its original signwriting and paint, it is often displayed at special events complete with rare Westfalia trailer for carrying long poles or pipes, usually supplied with a Pick-Up as SO 24 equipment.

The original signwriting is still in perfect condition as is the Ruby Red paint. Note the side flashers, standard on all buses exported to Italy.

Fitting a ladder rig to a Doka was prohibited in Germany due to weight restrictions.

A pole-mountable spotlight and hand pump extinguisher are sited just behind the cab.

A very rare Westfalia trailer for carrying long pipes and poles makes a period perfect accessory.

A Meyer-Hagen 10-metre wooden Ladder Truck conversion has been fitted to the load bed, making this the only Double Cab Ladder Truck known.

The Meyer-Hagen ladder is mounted on a removable frame, allowing the Pick-Up to function as a Crew Cab/load lugger.

This version also has no rear stabilizing feet, another feature illegal in Germany!

fire trucks (Feuerwehr)

1975 FIRST STRIKE FIRE TRUCK

This model was built in the UK on a Double Cab base by Brainbridge Fire and Security, Kent, and, along with a Tipper Truck and a Ladder Truck, was offered via VW UK dealerships. Only six models were known to have been produced; this is one of only two survivors. It was designed as a rapid response, fully equipped Fire Truck complete with water tanks, ladders and water pump. Carrying a crew of four, it was intended as first line defence for factories, small airfields, chemical works and so on.

A custom-built body, clad in sheet aluminium, was fitted onto the existing load bed, with roller blind access to storage and equipment, including a generator, on both sides. The rear of the vehicle has been extended to carry the Godiva pump and hoses and provide a standing area. A 23-foot (7m) steel ladder is carried on the roof along with twin blue flashing lights and two spotlights. The water tanks are slung under the chassis and can hold 100 gallons.

Built in 1975, it was not registered for use until 1980, when it was bought by Preston Health Authority and based at a psychiatric hospital. In 1997 it was decommissioned and acquired by a VW enthusiast.

The Brainbridge Fire Truck was based on a Double Cab and offered by VW UK through its dealerships.

BELOW: *A 23-foot (7m) steel ladder is carried on the roof, along with twin blue flashing lights and two spotlights.*

Only six models are known to have been produced, and this is one of only two survivors.

The rear of the vehicle has been extended to carry the Godiva pump and hoses and provide a standing area.

BELOW: The Double Cab base enabled it to carry a crew of four.

All the original fire-fighting equipment is intact and complete.

BELOW: A custom-built body, clad in sheet aluminium, was fitted onto the existing load bed, with roller blind access to storage and equipment, including a generator, on both sides.

fire trucks (Feuerwehr)

1986 SYNCRO FIRE SERVICE SUPPORT VAN

The bus is a standard 14-inch Syncro Windowed Van, with a 1900cc engine and fitted with a special order Dehler fixed high roof, with a window in the front section and special mouldings for mounting flashing lights. It was ordered in 1986 by the Wolfsburg City Fire Department and attached to the fire station for use as a back-up Personnel Transport/Rescue vehicle/ Ambulance. Finished in Fire Truck Red and White, it features the additional options of three blue flashing lights, four sirens, searchlight and roof indicators.

The 4WD Syncro was a perfect base vehicle in all terrains and weather.

It has been fitted with a special order Dehler high roof, featuring a window in the front section and special mouldings for the flashing lights.

LEFT: It still carries its original logos for use by Wolfsburg City Fire Department.

BELOW: It features the additional options of three blue flashing lights, four sirens, searchlight and roof indicators.

1986 FEUERWEHR DOUBLE CAB SYNCRO

The Double Cab was built in 1986 and delivered to the Kelkheim and Ruppertshain Freiwillige Feuerwehr (Volunteer Fire Brigade) near Frankfurt/Main for use as a personnel carrier. It is now back in service as Vanfest's own, on site, quick response fire fighting/first aid vehicle, with new equipment able to deal immediately with most emergencies. It is kitted out with the modern fire express system, which is lightweight and powerful. Apart from kitting out the Syncro with the fire express system and a custom-built two-hundred-litre water tank, the electrics have been split and an additional battery added. The full emergency kit also includes fire extinguishers, emergency tool kit with axes, first aid kit and burns kits and full

This 1986 ex-fire service Double Cab has been converted for use as Vanfest's own first reponse fire truck.

breathing apparatus. The load bed bay wooden side panels and floor have been fitted with aluminium chequer plate and a rear locker added, along

with an environmental spill kit, vehicle defibrillator and a red fibreglass ladder kit. A bull bar set up has been added to the front.

It is kitted out with the modern Fire Express System, which is lightweight and powerful.

The front bull bars are not original equipment but have been added by the Vanfest team.

It was originally used by a volunteer fire brigade in southern Germany as a personnel carrier.

It has seen use in its new role at Vanfest but, fortunately, it is mainly used for demonstration.

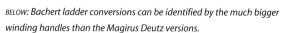

This 1957 Ladder Truck was fitted by Bachert with an extendable 10-metre (30-foot) metal ladder and was used as part of the Hoesch Hohenlimburg factory's fleet. Note the siren bank and detachable pole spotlight. Later style front flashers have been added beneath the headlights.

The Fire Service Gerätewagen (Tool and Equipment vehicle) was specially built to carry heavy tools and equipment, while the crew travelled separately. A large closed box was fabricated on a Single Cab base and roll-up steel blinds on either side (usually three on each side) gave access to separate shelved compartments and storage areas. Additional equipment could also be carried on the reinforced roof. The signwriting shows it was used in the Dietenheim/South Tyrol locality and it has been updated at some point with new front flashing indicators, siren and twin red flashing lights on the roof. Note the all-red bumpers and wheels.

The Panel Van sides and roof have been completely removed for easy all-round access to the pump on this 1958 Fire Truck owned by the Cristal Brewery in Belgium.

This Dutch-converted mobile pump Fire Truck was a twin cargo door model for flexible access. Built in 1959/60, it features a specially designed roof rack to carry long hoses and windows in each side door. The pump unit had to be lifted out by hand.

Built on 24 October 1961 (#847847) this saw service with the voluntary fire brigade in the Idstein district. In addition to the usual mobile pump unit Fire Truck spec, it also had factory-fitted flashing headlights (M19), mud and snow tyres (M101) and larger oil bath air cleaner (M156). Supplied by Bachert, it features an extendable wooden ladder carried on the roof in a purpose-built rack. Note the maker's name on the engine lid.

Many northern Italian Alpine regions used VW-based Fire Trucks as they were easy to manoeuvre in difficult terrain. Note the full-length roof rack and emergency spotlight-mounting pole on the front of this 1961 Double Cab version. Clear indicator lenses were Italian spec until the 1970s.

This 1961 Dutch Crew Transport/Mobile Pump Unit has been adapted from a Panel Van and a window cut into each cargo door. The rear has been closed off for carrying equipment with an open access cut into the side. The pump and hose are transported on a trailer.

Used by the Lauerbach voluntary fire brigade, this 1963 Pick-Up carries a 600 metre (2,000 feet) hose and all its couplings and connectors. Known as a Schlauchwagen SW 600 (Large Hose Transporter), it is finished in the red and white paint scheme used to make it more visible to other drivers.

Built in Italy, this Fire Truck conversion was based on a 1964 twin cargo door Kombi. It was used as a personnel carrier with the inside fitted out with wood slat benches. Fitted with an Italian rbe and full tone siren it also carries a pair of wooden ladders on the roof and a searchlight at the rear.

fire trucks (Feuerwehr)

The Dry Powder Fire Truck was vital for fires where water was ineffective or dangerous. This version, built in 1965, features the standard option of twin sliding doors (M162) and the 250kg dry powder equipment was supplied and fitted by TOTAL UK.

This 1971 Single Cab has been converted to become a fully operational fire-fighting unit known as a Betriebsfeuerwehr (Fire Equipment vehicle). Pump, hoses, ladders and tools are mounted in specially designed carrying frames on the load bed and sides.

Larger municipal fire services also had a range of specialist vehicles, such as this 1971 Cherry Picker, which was ideal for both rescue and using hoses at window height.

Panel Vans were also fitted with roof ladders in special racks as on this 1973 version. Note the raised front bumper with integral fog lights and twin blue lights.

This 1977 Gerätewagen version, with roof ladders, was based on a Pick-Up and formed part of Volkswagen's own factory emergency response fleet.

This Wolfsburg factory-equipped T3 was built in 1980, one of the last mobile pump VW built and equipped versions.

First response crew vehicles with ladders and pump continued on the T3 base as in this 1981 KEF (small action vehicle) used in Stuttgart.

By the late 1980s Volkswagens were used more for personnel transport as in this 1987 Mannschaftswagen based on a Caravelle C and used in Lower Saxony.

This T3 Double Cab Fire Truck was based in the Taunus Centre shopping complex, where height was restricted. Note the low position of the blue lights for access to the complex car parks.

Members of the Wolfsburg Fire Department practising emergency call out in the late 1980s.

T4 Fire Command and Coordination unit (Berufsfeuerwehr), based in Berlin.

This LWB T3 Command vehicle features a factory half high roof option.

hearse conversions (Leichenwagen)

ABOVE: 1963 Frickinger and 1964 Pollmann Hearses.

Hearse conversions were available from the early 1950s, with several small companies such as Pollmann producing versions. By the 1960s specialist funeral transport coachbuilders Frickinger specialized in Volkswagen-based conversions. Although not an official SO model, dealership catalogues from 1963 included information about the models, which were ordered and supplied directly from Frickinger.

ABOVE: This 1956 Panel Van conversion was built by an unknown Austrian converter. It featured two large side windows, a large tailgate window and deluxe beltline trim. The bullet indicators are a later modification.

LEFT: This archive photograph shows a 1955 Panel Van conversion, with no side doors. Carried out by Vögtle and Zeller of Freiburg, it features two, windowless, coachbuilt rear doors and deluxe trim.

FRICKINGER CONVERSIONS

Frickinger maker's badge.

The Double Cab Frickinger had an extended rear section to accommodate the coffin.

The firm of Fritz Frickinger, based in Augsburg, started making funeral cars in the 1930s, and in the mid 1950s began converting VW Buses for use by municipal authorities, mortuaries and private funeral firms. Early versions were Panel Vans with large glass windows fitted and a platform running from the engine bay shelf to the bulkhead and featured deluxe chrome trim. From the early 1960s Frickinger offered two versions – one built on a Kombi or Panel, and another version that used a Pick-Up (or Double Cab) with a new enclosed coachbuilt steel frame spot welded to the cab and load area.

The Panel Van and Kombi versions had factory partitions between the cab and load areas, and a new load platform made from tubular steel and plywood was installed and faced with vinyl or sheet metal. Coffins were secured by fitted hooks, and side walls and roof were lined with aluminium, though white vinyl was optional for the roof. A drainage channel for body fluids was sited behind the right-hand side door leading to a holding tank and a similar body fluid channel was by the rear hatch. The Pick-Up was supplied without side gates and a new coachwork frame was spot welded to the cab and load bed to enclose the base. The interior was finished as for the Panel Van and rear access was via twin loading doors. A Double Cab version was also available, and featured an extended rear coffin load area that overhung at the rear.

Both versions featured a ventilator and air extractor built into the roof, along with a lattice-covered roof light.

Most Frickingers used Pick-Up bases with a coachbuilt enclosed rear area with twin door access.

This 1972 T2 version was originally used as a Mortuary Van.

The aluminium-clad inside is utilitarian with plain wooden runners.

hearse conversions (Leichenwagen)

The two rectangular side windows had chrome trim and frosted glass, with an etched design usually featuring a cross and two sloping palms; purple curtains were optional. Protective bars were fitted inside to each window.

The exterior was finished in black acrylic enamel, with polished aluminium belt trim and an additional 40mm side trim, all with black rubber centre sections. Plastic chrome trim was added all round the roof gutter and the front badge was either silver or chrome. Bumpers and hubcaps were painted silver; chrome versions were also an option.

1972 FRICKINGER

The Bay Window model featured here is a 1972 Single Cab, supplied without side gates to the Frickinger Karosserie for conversion and use as an Undertaker's Van for delivering and collecting bodies from mortuaries and attending traffic accidents. Frickinger's Bay models differ from the Split Screen versions as the enclosed frame round the load bed is made from moulded fibreglass not steel and rear access is via a top hinged single door with no window. Cab windows had chrome trim surrounds, and polished aluminium trim with black inserts was fitted around the front half of the body, under the windows. Further trim was fitted at the original load bed height, extending onto the cab doors, and black bumpers were standard.

BELOW: Bay models differ from the Split Screen versions as the enclosed frame round the load bed is made from moulded fibreglass, not steel, and rear access is via a top hinged single door.

The Hearse was repainted in VW Candy White and new logos, featuring a dove, applied to the sides and tailgate for a softer and less sombre touch.

The original Pick-Up base can be clearly seen from the cooling vents and 'treasure chest'.

BELOW: The frosted windows have been replaced with clear glass and the tailgate fitted with a clear glass window so the coffin and floral tributes can be seen by family and friends.

RIGHT: Polished aluminium trim with black inserts was fitted around the front half of the body, under the windows and also at the original load bed height, extending onto the cab doors.

The refurbished interior, finished in burgundy, features a new polished wood coffin deck that looks more professional than the original, utilitarian metal lining.

After mortuary service in Germany it was used by the Belgian undertaker Robert, whose signwriting was still on the vehicle when Clare Brookes and Michelle Orton acquired it from BBT in August 2007. They already ran a successful VW Wedding Transport business and had been looking for a suitable vehicle to use for funerals, and a purpose-built VW version was just perfect!

They have fully restored the Hearse, adding a new polished wood coffin deck that looks more professional than the original utilitarian metal lining and wood runners. The frosted windows have been replaced with clear glass and the tailgate fitted with a clear glass window so the coffin and floral tributes can be seen by family and friends. The inside has been finished in burgundy. The Hearse was then repainted in VW Candy White, to match the rest of the fleet. New logos featuring a dove, the symbol of peace, have been applied to the sides and tailgate and a black pennant flag has been added to the roof.

An all-white VW Hearse may seem strange to some, but it seems softer and less sombre without detracting from the sadness or grief the passing of a loved one brings, plus it is also less disturbing for children. This is probably now the only classic VW Hearse still in service. (More information can be found at www.volkswagenfunerals. co.uk)

THE POLLMAN HEARSE

The firm of Pollmann in Bremen also specialized in coachbuilt hearses. Early versions used a Panel Van base but, from 1959, they were built on Single and Double Cab base models (the load bed was lengthened by 60 cm on Doka versions). Twin opening doors were fitted into a specially fabricated steel body, which was seamlessly grafted to the Double Cab roof and sides. Two coffins could be carried. Finished in black with silver-painted bumpers and hubcaps, the body featured deluxe trim on the front panel with additional chrome trim round the bed line, roof and windows. Side windows had an etched leaf pattern and, optionally, rear door windows a cross. White lamps were also fitted on each side of the long window.

TOP LEFT: Based on a Panel Van, this 1958 version has deluxe trim, reshaped to run under the new side windows, and two windows in the rear doors. TOP RIGHT: Finished in black with silver-painted bumpers and hubcaps, this Pollmann, based on a Pick-Up, featured deluxe trim on the front panel with additional chrome trim round the bed line, roof and windows, as seen in these factory photographs from May 1959.

ABOVE: Twin opening doors were fitted into a specially fabricated steel body, which was seamlessly grafted to the Double Cab roof and sides.
RIGHT: Side windows had an etched leaf pattern and white lamps were fitted on each side.

1964 POLLMAN

The base model for this Pollmann Hearse was a 1964 Double Cab Pick-Up, one of only ten made. Initially it was used by the undertakers Matthias Vogel, whose chromed twin bars and MV logo are still badged on the front in chrome. It then saw service with various undertakers in Karlsruhe until 1986, when it passed into private ownership. The original frosted side windows remain but the chrome trim and white lamps that were fitted fore and aft of the windows are now missing, and it has also been repainted in aubergine. After being used as a Camper for several years, it has been put into store awaiting restoration. Note the changed rear door window shape from the 1959 version.

Pollmann continue to offer Hearse conversions on the VW base, as in this 1993 T4 conversion.

1980 RAPPOLD HEARSE

This T3 funeral car, based on a silver Panel Van, was converted in 1980 by Eugen Rappold of Wülfrath and designed to be more elegant and dignified than other models. The base model had a host of factory options including cab sunroof, laminated glass, heated windscreen, locking fuel cap, double passenger seat, heavy-duty shock absorbers and generator, head restraints and bad weather package. The conversion included black leatherette for the roof, full-length windows cut into the sides and modified tailgate with large window. The load area has a slide-out frame for easy loading/unloading of coffins, black drapes to each side window, buttoned leatherette lining to the cab partition and sides and ornate coach lamps topped with crucifixes. It is now part of the Bulli Museum collection in Hessisch Oldendorf.

The Rappold Hearse was designed to be more elegant and dignified than other models.

The conversion included black leatherette for
the roof.

*RIGHT: Full-length windows were cut into the sides and a
modified tailgate with large window fitted.*

*LEFT: The interior features slide-out frame, black drapes to each side window,
buttoned leatherette lining, and ornate coach lamps topped with crucifixes.*

*BELOW: Despite the 'windows', the inside is actually closed, lined in mahogany
and has a slide-out coffin platform.*

T5 HEARSE

*This T5 Hearse conversion by Kuhlmann is based on a Panel Van and
features a pick-up style 'treasure chest' and large red-tinted windows
with etched sunburst design for a contemporary funeral car styling.*

ABOVE: 1978 Follow Me Van leading a C-130 Hercules as it taxes on an airbase in Germany.

The VW Bus was used extensively by the military, notably in Holland, Switzerland and Norway, as well as Germany, with diverse functions ranging from mobile field kitchens to airbase Follow Me Vans. Mainly they were standard models, often featuring Eberspächer heater and limited slip options, and only required painting in camouflage khaki, drab olive or grey, with the addition of military fittings such as black out, generator sockets and securing brackets for rail transport. The most common uses were as Personnel Transport or Mobile Radio Units.

1966 SWISS ARMY COMMAND COMMUNICATIONS VEHICLE

The versatility and ruggedness of the VW Bus made it an ideal Mobile Command and Radio Unit. This Kombi,

A military specification rack for transporting the antenna was bolted directly onto the roof. Note the extra vent panel in the rear upper corner for the generator.

Close-up of the reinforced armour antenna mounting plate over tha cab roof.

Military models featured a front-facing convoy light to facilitate stealth nighttime travel.

ABOVE: The rear hatch has an exhaust and sliding hatch used for inspection of the running generator.

LEFT: Military vehicle specification included under-chassis securing brackets for rail transport.

affectionately now known as the Battle Bus, rolled off the production line in May 1966 destined for the Swiss army. In order to cope with tracks and off-road conditions it was factory fitted with low ratio (Alpine) gears (M092) and a limited slip differential (M220). Having the low ratio gearbox, it was also fitted with a speed governor and speedometer that displays red warning lines to prevent over-revving. The Swiss army also added a yellow warning sign adjacent to the speedometer advising a 70km/h (45mph) maximum speed.

It was used as a Command vehicle and was equipped with the SE222 Funkstation (radio) and associated

The cab area is sealed from the load area with a sliding window partition with its own roll-down black out blind.

equipment. The Command vehicles were used for communications between the temporary bases and serving armoured vehicles and troops in the field. Originally the interior of

this van would have been fitted with the SE222 Funkstation, along with a large map table for plotting. The front cab had a small fold-down map desk. A generator was situated in the back

Rifle racks were standard fittings.

Anti-grenade bars were fitted to the pop-out windows. All windows could be fitted with black-out boards, held by steel clips fitted to the window edges.

screen covered the front cab. Ventilation is provided by standard rear pop-out windows; however, the military specification would include anti-grenade steel 'jail' bars.

On the roof is a reinforced armour plating section that seats the heavy-duty antenna, which is over 10 feet (3m) tall. When dismantled, it was carried in a tube on the military specification roof rack. The equipment carried by these command post vans also included an earthing stake, used to reduce the risk of electrocution of the operators when set up stationary in the field. Red warning signs regarding the removal of the antenna are also fixed to the cargo and driver's doors. As is commonplace with Swiss military vehicles, this van has an addition of a front-facing convoy light to facilitate stealth nighttime travel. The Radio Van would have carried the radio operator and driver and a former operator of this vehicle said that these vehicles did not get a lot of use during service; the most used component was the ashtrays!

section above the engine bay to power the radio equipment. The generator was separated from the cargo area by a steel firewall. The rear hatch has an exhaust and sliding hatch used for inspection of the running generator. The cargo area of the van would have had the ability to 'black out' to the outside world when operating at night with the use of ridged board black-out screens. These boards cover the windows, held by steel clips fitted to the window edges, and a roll-down

The van was sold in 1998 to a Swiss-Italian from Biasca, who used it to gather wood from the forest. In December 2003 it was sold on in Austria before eventually ending up in the hands of a Volkswagen collector and dealer in Belgium. The current owners, David Hyde and Kerra Shaw, acquired it in July 2004 with just 36,000 kilometres (22,500 miles) on the odometer.

1962 SWISS ARMY FIELD SERVICE VEHICLE

This version of a side flap SO 1 conversion was carried out by the Swiss army, but based on a Kombi instead of a Panel Van. Designed as a field service/repair vehicle, it was built in 1962 and delivered without rear seating (M013). The major body modification was to turn the three-side window panel into a hinged flap, with lower flap-down section. This large opening side panel made for easy access to tools, documents and spare parts.

On the bulkhead behind the driver, electrical testing equipment had been fitted for testing headlight bulbs and batteries. The van runs on 6V, but it also has a 12V battery installed to allow testing of 12V headlight bulbs; a switch allows movement between the two voltage systems. Heavy-duty metal drawer units have been fitted to the inside area accessed from behind the side flap and from the rear tailgate. Opening wooden traps inside the side flap give access to large spaces where wax oil, engine oil and transmission fluid were stored. Behind the upright

opening door is the document filing cupboard, which would carry the technical details and service records of the military vehicles tended too. Inside the cargo doors a small workbench with a work vice allowed simple repairs in the field. Other repairs would include welding and tyre changing. Twelve-volt strip lights have been fitted to the roof over both side openings; this enabled nighttime work to take place. Another typical military necessity was the addition of a front-facing convoy light to facilitate stealth night time travel.

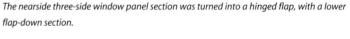

This side service flap Kombi was designed as a mobile workshop/breakdown vehicle.

The nearside three-side window panel section was turned into a hinged flap, with a lower flap-down section.

This large opening side panel made for easy access to tools, documents and spare parts. Note the capital 'P' on the military identification plate, fitted front and rear of the vehicle, indicating this to be an AMP (Army Motor Park) pool vehicle.

Heavy-duty metal drawer units are fitted to the inside area behind the side flap, and wooden trapdoors inside the side flap are for storing bulky items.

LEFT: On the bulkhead behind the driver, electrical testing equipment for testing headlight bulbs and batteries is fitted.

RIGHT: Pigeonhole compartments carry documentation, handbooks and repair manuals

BELOW LEFT: The inside is divided centrally with the cargo door side used for the workshop.

BELOW RIGHT: As well as tools and a bench with vice there is a 12V battery for testing equipment; a switch moves it back to using the original 6V system.

Military vehicles that this van supported included the Willys Jeep, Hanomag-Henschel 7 and 8 tonne trucks, Saurer 2DM and Berna 2VM (4 x 4) 4,500kg trucks, the Mercedes Unimog and Sanitätswagen (Ambulance).

Known in the Swiss army as an AMP (Army Motor Park) pool vehicle – indicated by the capital 'P' on the military identification plate, fitted front and rear of the vehicle – it was based between the four Swiss military centres at Hinwil, Uthmarsingen, Rothernburg and Thun. When it was

decommissioned is unknown, but it was discovered in a disused airbase in West Germany that was being cleared. A Volkswagen dealer from the UK bought the van in 2007 and added signwriting, amended the colour of the bumpers and made one or two other changes. The van was used to sell parts and accessories for the business. The current owners, David Hyde and Kerra Shaw, purchased the van from him in October 2009, and after making it roadworthy, now attend shows and events with it along with their ex-Swiss army Radio Van.

Similar side flap conversions were carried out and used by the Swiss army on Bay Window Kombis.

BELOW: Two wheels with mud and snow tyres and fuel cans were also carried in the load compartment/workshop area.

The Dutch army made extensive use of Kemperink conversions.

Now a Camper with side windows added, this version was originally a Radio Van and is still in its original army livery.

KEMPERINK MILITARY CONVERSIONS

1966 DUTCH RADIO VAN

The Dutch army used Kemperinks for a variety of purposes including Radio Vans and field kitchens. This 1966 Kemperink was originally used as a Mobile Radio Field Unit and Control Centre by the Dutch army. It still has its original army paint, side reflectors, Dutch flag logo and generator/cable access panels but has been converted into a Camper and side windows have been added.

RIGHT ABOVE: Note the additional side and rear reflectors and Dutch flag insignia on the left rear by the engine lid.

RIGHT BELOW: A Kemperink fitted with sales flap/serving counter in use by the Dutch army on manoeuvres in 1962.

NORWEGIAN ARMY CATERING BUS

This 1967 example, used by the Norwegian army as a mobile field kitchen, is a standard Westfalia SO 2, featuring the original glass-fronted display/serving counter and special full-length roof rack.

This Australian Model Box Van was used in the 1960s by the Australian army as a mobile base for measuring bomb blasts tested in the outback.

It was fully restored in 2009 and given a custom makeover including drop spindles, Mango Green/Off White paint, and Australian-style mesh sun visor.

It is now owned by Brian Bussell and used as a mobile Mexican fast food van.

AUSTRALIAN ARMY BOX VAN

The Box or Container Van was an Australian special body conversion, built at the Clayton factory. Unlike the German Box Van special model, which was based on a Pick-Up, the Australian version was based on a Panel Van but gave additional load capacity (*see* page 000). The version here was built in 1964 and was used by the Australian army as a mobile base for measuring bomb blasts tested in the Outback.

Brian Bussell brought it to the UK in 2009, whereupon it was given a custom makeover prior to being reborn as a mobile cooked food van. It was lowered at the front with T2D drop spindles, lowered slightly at the back, a CSP brake disc conversion fitted and up-rated to 12V, with electric hook-up and inverter fitted to run all the kitchen equipment. It was then re-sprayed in VW Mango Green and Off White and personalized with new signwriting to advertise the new business, Chilli Gone Barmy. It now attends events and festivals.

Chilli Gone Barmy attends events and festivals (pictured here at Stanford Hall) where it is always a hit, appreciated especially by hungry bus-buffers.

The mobile aircraft scrambler, based on a Double Door Panel Van, featured a glass observation tower.

The vehicle was used by the RAAF to deploy Mirage jet fighters and F-111s to battle or on exercise. Officially designated 'AF/MRC-802 Mobile Strip Operations Telebriefing System', the unit was informally known as the 'Hot Telebrief' or 'Telescrambler'.

THE TELESCRAMBLER ROYAL AUSTRALIAN AIRFORCE MOBILE STRIP OPERATIONS UNIT (SOP)

1967 DOUBLE DOOR CONTROL TOWER BUS

In order to meet their need for a mobile, hot scramble control unit able to deploy quickly to either end of the airstrip depending on wind conditions, the Royal Australian Airforce (RAAF) decided to convert a 1967 Double Door Panel Van into a Mobile Strip Operations (SOP) Unit. (It had previously been used as a Follow Me aircraft parking vehicle, as shown by the original chequered black and yellow paint work found under the later GSE Yellow during restoration.) It was converted by the RAAF over eighteen months in 1971/72 by GEMS at No 1 AD, Laverton, with communications and operator equipment fitted by TIMS at No 1 AD. Although built in 1967, it featured the pre-1963 smaller tailgate and twin cooling vents in the upper side panel as found on Clayton (VW Australia's plant) built buses. Officially designated 'AF/MRC-802 Mobile Strip Operations Telebriefing System', the unit was

informally known as the 'Hot Telebrief' or 'Telescrambler'. While several RAAF Kombis were converted for similar service, this is the only one known to have been built with this style of glass observation tower.

The vehicle was used to deploy Mirage jet fighters and F-111s to battle or on exercise. The full system also utilized a trailer, which carried the air conditioning and generator units. Cool air was ducted into the rear of the van and out through louvres located in the box section on the roof. A large diameter flexible hose that connected with a quarter turn was fitted to a mounting section at the rear of the box section and connected to the AC trailer unit to provide necessary cool air in the tropical clime of northern Australia.

Apart from all the necessary interior communications, UHF/AM transceivers and radar equipment, the body had extensive modifications made to suit its new role. The cargo area was totally enclosed and insulated against jet noise, and a large double-glazed glass observation roof tower was fitted onto a reinforced box section fixed to the roof with the existing roof panel cut away to allow access for operators, who sat on raised chairs inside. To aid

visibility, twin sunroofs had already been fitted over the front cab area, as with all RAAF airfield vehicles. A fixed ladder gave access to a small observation platform mounted at the rear of the base and the roof mounting points for six aerials. Two small hatches were cut into the rear on either side of the tailgate to allow access for various cables. The air conditioning duct was mounted on a box section at the rear of the roof platform. It was painted in GSE Yellow (Ground Service Equipment Yellow), which is still used for all ground equipment on military airfields. On both sides of the swage line were small securing rings, which were used to anchor the vehicle to protect it from swaying in the jet engine slipstream. As well as direct communication with the pilots, additional telephone lines kept the unit in contact with the control tower and operations commander. Because of aircraft noise, a powerful PA system was used to keep ground crew informed and briefed. (This PA system had to be tested each day and, apparently, 'going to test the air con system or the PA' was a good way for a technician to grab five minutes' peace, with a handy telephone to warn if an officer was on the way!)

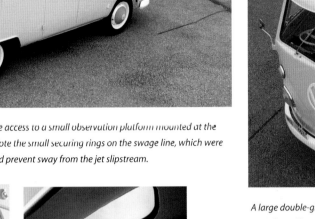

A fixed ladder gave access to a small observation platform mounted at the rear of the base. Note the small securing rings on the swage line, which were used to anchor and prevent sway from the jet slipstream.

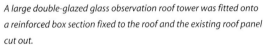

A large double-glazed glass observation roof tower was fitted onto a reinforced box section fixed to the roof and the existing roof panel cut out.

FAR LEFT: The operators sat on raised swivel chairs to use the radio and radar equipment and to watch over proceedings.

LEFT: To aid visibility, twin sunroofs were fitted over the front cab area (a modification on all RAAF airstrip vehicles).

Now known, and signwritten, as 'Los Scramblas Café' the bus is currently used to serve up classic Mexican dishes. Though built in 1967, it features the pre-1963 smaller tailgate and Australian spec twin cooling vents in the upper side panel as found on Clayton-built buses.

It saw service at Amberley base between 1973 and 1979 until modern technology made it obsolete and it was stripped of its equipment and left to stand in an airforce scrap yard in Darwin. There it sat until 2001, when Andre Hummel happened upon it. As an army pilot with a love of classic Kombis, he immediately realized it was something a bit special and worth saving. Most of the equipment, such as the emergency portable runway lighting, PA system, UHF-AM radio, communications equipment and sets, amplifiers, microphones, warning horn, radio vibrators and buzzers had been removed, but the stand on which the two controllers sat, the radio tray and the circuit breaker panel were still intact. After protracted negotiations with the aviation scrap yard, he finally rescued the bus and spent the next year restoring and rebuilding it from the ground up, refurbishing all the roof fittings and interior and repainting it in GSE Yellow. The finished vehicle was used as a daily driver from 2004 until 2008, when it passed into the hands of Luke Bridgewater, who was looking for an iconic vehicle to use in a new mobile fast food venture. Known now as 'Los Scramblas Café' the bus serves up classic Mexican dishes using locally sourced and organic ingredients and, unsurprisingly, attracts attention wherever it goes.

RIGHT: This was how it looked in 2001, when it was discovered languishing in an aviation scrap yard. The box section at the rear of the roof platform was for ducting cool air from an accompanying trailer unit.

electric-powered transporters

ABOVE: A 1972 demonstration vehicle is now in the Stiftung AutoMuseum, Wolfsburg.

Volkswagen began experimental work with electric battery-powered Transporters in the late 1960s and one of the prototypes was designed jointly with Bosch, Varta and the Rheinisch-Westfälische AG Power Company in 1972/73, based on a Kombi.

Around seventy versions of electric-powered Type 2s were built, and models on a Kombi, Panel Van or Pick-Up base could be ordered from German VW dealerships. The Ben Pon dealership in Holland also offered the electric-powered version. Twin sliding door models were preferred as they provided easier access to the slide-out battery bank. The additional weight and space meant the payload was reduced to 800kg. The rear-sited Siemens-built DC motor provided 17kW (23bhp) continuous power, 33.5kW

1972 Gas Turbine prototype and 1978 Electric-Powered Panel Van on display at the 60th Anniversary International Volkswagen Bus Convention in Hanover.

This 1978 Electric-Powered T2 was based on a Panel Van and was kitted out with heavy-duty lifting gear. The signwriting reads 'We drive with electricity, in an environmentally friendly manner.' It now resides in the T2 Bulli Museum.

A 1972 prototype gas turbine-powered version used an engine similar to jet aircraft.

This Late Bay prototype electric conversion was made in Holland and differs from the others in that the whole cargo area is filled with the batteries and equipment, instead of in a slide-out tray. As such it was more an experimental project than practical application.

(45bhp) peak power and 160Nm of torque. The forces flowed through a single-stage gearbox to the rear wheels (no clutch) and the vehicle was capable of 0–50km/h (0–30mph) in 12s and could cruise at 70km/h (40mph). The powerful lead battery was sited on a slide-out tray under a reinforced load bed in the cargo area, and was capable of storing power to give a 50- to 80-kilometre range. The battery alone weighed 850kg; with the added floor and chassis strengthening the van weighed in at just 2.2 tonnes, necessitating the fitting of heavy-duty special shock absorbers. Additional cooling vents were cut into the sliding doors to stop overheating in the battery compartment.

Volkswagen also developed a hybrid drive version with standard engine and hydrodynamic converter/electro pneumatic clutch and, in 1972, also built a gas turbine-powered version, using an engine similar to jet aircraft. This proved very inefficient, however, and the project was abandoned, though the prototype still exists in the Volkswagen museum. A demonstration model of one of the hybrid drive vehicles, known as the City Taxi, toured the USA in 1973 and was a guest at several exhibitions, including the Museum of Modern Art in New York.

In 1978 the Tennessee Valley Power Authority ordered a test fleet of ten electric vehicles, and in Wolfsburg, from 1979 to 1984, about fifty electric vehicles on the T3 base were built. In the 1990s a small fleet of twelve hybrid drive LTs were tested by the Bundespost, but never went into production.

BACK TO THE FUTURE: THE CHAMELEON

ELECTRIC CONCEPT MICROBUS

In February 2006 Volkswagen of America's Electronic Research Lab (ERL), in California's Silicon Valley, decided to showcase its latest electronic wizardry. They sourced a rusty 1964 Deluxe Microbus, which they saw as the ultimate icon of cool, christened it 'the Chameleon', and contracted LeVere's Volkswagen Restoration to carry out a bare metal restoration and re paint in Titian Red/Beige Grey. Before delivery, Hybrid Technologies installed the

Surfboards carried on the roof racks have flexible solar panels installed within them to aid charging.

In place of the horn-button on the steering wheel is a touch pad that controls the sound system, navigation and wide-angle rear parking camera. A computer display screen is installed where the speedometer once resided.

LED front and rear lights are manufactured by Osram-Sylvania.

In the middle of the rear bumper is a small screen that is a personalized 'bumper sticker', which allows you to program in your own messages to display on its screen.

latest all-electric engine, running on ten 30V lithium-polymer batteries, giving the bus a range of 100 miles (160km). Recharging is carried out by hooking up a power lead to a plug located where the exhaust tail pipe would originally have been located. Surfboards carried on the roof racks have flexible solar panels installed within them to aid charging.

After a new paint job the interior was re-trimmed as close to original spec as possible and California Concepts hooked up all the electronic gadgets using 'hidden technology'. An impressive list includes voice-activated MP3 entertainment system and motorized 60-inch projection screen fitted behind the cab seats. In place of the horn-button on the steering wheel is a touch pad, which controls

the sound, navigation and wide-angle rear-parking camera. A special feature computer screen is installed where the speedometer once resided. Other touches include the LED front and rear lights from Osram-Sylvania and in the middle of the rear bumper is a small screen, which is a personalized 'bumper sticker' – you program in your own messages to display on its screen. Locking and unlocking of the doors is done via a palm vein recognition system, hidden behind the petrol flap.

In May 2006 the bus travelled back to Germany for an in-house technology show before making its public debut at the Boston Alternative Transportation Festival in September 2006.

THE FUTURE?

Current Volkswagen research and development is focused on BlueMotion fuel-efficient engines, though hybrid drive and electric models have not been discounted entirely, especially as major competitors start to

unveil viable versions. At the 2010 Internationale Automobil-Ausstellung (IAA), Dr Wolfgang Schreiber, CEO for VW Commercial Vehicles, stated that an electric version of the Caddy, the E-Caddy, will be fleet-tested in Hanover during 2011, and that by the end of 2011, or early 2012, a T5 Plug-in Hybrid with a range of 800 to 1,000 kilometres (500–620 miles) will be tested as well. Hybrid drive and electric models could be ready for serial production at earliest from 2013 onwards.

In early 2011 at the Motor Show in Geneva, VW Passenger Car division unveiled its latest Concept Car – an all-electric MPV. Badged with the iconic BULLI name, the vehicle is fully electric with a minimalist interior, features twin three-seater bench seats and has all functions centred on the latest iPad technology. Despite PR associations with the name Bulli and Transporters/Campers, this clearly is no load-lugging workhorse, and for styling draws heavily on the 2002 Concept Microbus shown at Detroit. But it is a glimpse into the future …

An electric concept MPV known as the Bulli, premiered at the Geneva Motor Show in 2011.

index

The VW Transporter Sonderschau Tour in 1962 featured a Ladder Truck, Deluxe Microbus, Cherry Picker, Tipper, Ambulance, Fire truck, Police Accident Unit, Low loader, Sales Flap shop, Freezer Van and Koffer-Aufbau (Container van).

Amongst the many models exhibited at the 60 Year Bus Anniversary celebrations in Hanover 2007 were a Police Loudspeaker/Riot Control Bus, various fire truck conversions, a Pick-Up with crane lift, Doka and pole-carrying trailer and one of the original Plattenwagens (top right).